ALAN SHEARER

MY ILLUSTRATED CAREER

ALAN SHEARER

MY ILLUSTRATED CAREER

CASSELL
ILLUSTRATED

CONTENTS

FOREWORD

I didn't know Alan Shearer properly before I became the manager of Newcastle United but he certainly knew how to make an instant impression. In our first home game together, we beat Sheffield Wednesday 8-0 with Alan scoring five of the goals!

It was a dream start for us, and Alan continued to be a dream for the rest of my time at St James' Park, both as a player and as a person. What started as an excellent working relationship developed over time into a really good friendship as well.

I'd met Alan once, briefly, before 1999 when I was a guest of honour at an England match. I'd also tried to sign him around Euro '96 when I was at Barcelona and he was at Blackburn Rovers.

He became one of the first few players I tried to buy when I became coach at Barcelona but Blackburn Rovers immediately put up a 'not for sale sign'. I was pleased with this decision when I joined him at St James' Park three years later!

Alan also turned down Manchester United to sign for Newcastle even though he knew silverware was virtually guaranteed at Old Trafford. It endeared him to the Geordie public and they worshipped him from then onwards.

As a player and captain, I found him a massive example to his team-mates, in the dressing room as well as on the pitch.

He was a talisman and has this 'aura' about him without being arrogant.

When he had his say, everyone listened. His opinions were always sound and insightful and, as a manager, it's great when you have a captain singing from the same hymn sheet. I just wish I could have had half-a-dozen Alan Shearers in my team – in terms of ability and attitude. We would have beaten everyone then!

People often ask me, what made Alan Shearer so great? It was because he had so many different qualities, as a leader and as a striker.

He had the tremendous strength of character and mental toughness you associate with a Patrick Vieira or Roy Keane. But was also a fantastic centre-forward, which is the hardest position on the pitch in my opinion.

Some strikers are great in the air. Others are terrific finishers. They can also be good tacklers, have a good first touch, or be able to chase lost causes and turn bad passes into good ones. Alan Shearer had all those qualities – and that is extremely rare indeed. This may sound strange to people not in the game but I was always impressed with the way he could convert headers whether the crosses came in from the left or right. Look closely at some strikers, they are better from one side or the other. Alan was lethal from either flank.

I had the great fortune to manage some truly awe-inspiring leaders. Terry Butcher, Tony Adams, Stuart Pearce and Bryan Robson spring to mind. The highest compliment I can pay Alan is that no-one was better than him.

In addition, he was a perfect role model, to his team-mates and 'his people', the Geordie nation.

Alan, you were a phenomenal player and a true credit to your profession on and off the field. No wonder both your club and your country have found it so hard to replace you.

SIR BOBBY ROBSON

INTRODUCTION

Often it has been suggested that I am a very single-minded – even bloody-minded – individual. I wouldn't argue with that. As a striker you have to be firm, determined and focused totally on your goals. I have always stuck firmly to those ideals during my life.

And not just on the pitch. I have had to make some big decisions during my football career and I can honestly say I have made them all without any regrets. Often they have brought criticism my way.

The one thing that is always thrown at me is that I have won only a single major honour – the Premiership title when I was at Blackburn. People are only too keen to point out that I should have a cupboard full of medals to go with my goal-scoring achievements. They will add that if I had chosen a different route when it came to moving clubs I would have a collection of trophies to match anyone's in the domestic game.

What they are implying is that I should have joined Manchester United when I had the chance. It is true that I could have moved to Old Trafford on a couple of occasions but both times I turned the opportunity down – firstly to join Blackburn when I left Southampton and then when I quit Rovers to join Newcastle United.

I will go into the reasons in some detail later in the book, but for now I will just say that I would take exactly the same decisions if I had the chance to make them again. No regrets – definitely not.

During my retirement season, I was honoured at a tribute dinner during which Sir Alex Ferguson was good enough to say a few kind words about me. Those close to me will know that we have not always been on each other's Christmas card lists, probably because I snubbed him twice.

But on this occasion he was glowing in his praise for me. He could not resist, however, pointing out that if I had chosen to sign for United I would have ended up winning a lot more prizes. He was right, but I could not help saying in my response: 'Yes, Sir Alex, but if I had agreed to join United, you would have won a whole lot more as well!'

I am more than content that I can look back on a career that has satisfied all my boyhood ambitions – with the exception, of course, of winning a trophy with my beloved Newcastle United. I have lived my dreams and a few nightmares, but I feel fulfilled in every sense.

I haven't always done what people have expected me to do. For example, when I was a fresh-faced teenager I decided to move to the other end of the country to sign for Southampton rather than wait to receive an offer from my hometown club. I did so because I wanted to learn how to stand on my own two feet without having the home comforts I would have enjoyed by staying on Tyneside.

Once I got over my homesickness, I grew up quickly and learned how to fend for myself. I could make my own decisions even before I had left school. I always remember when my dad was first approached by the Southampton scout Jack Hixon, who asked whether I fancied going to The Dell for trials. Dad responded: 'Ask him yourself. He is old enough to make up his own mind.'

I did not need to be asked twice. I had already set my heart on being a footballer. Nothing more mattered in my life apart from my family who never stood in the way of chasing my dream, even if at times it was at the expense of my schoolwork. I would not say I was thick but I was never a great academic. For me school was a means to go and have a laugh with my mates – and play football, whether it was in organised matches or kicking a ball around in the playground.

Looking back I don't think I could have had a better further education than I did by leaving school early and moving to the south coast. Even if I had stayed on at school and gone to university – and there was precious little chance of that happening – I would not have had a better opportunity to prepare myself for adulthood.

Southampton Football Club was my university. There, I learned not only my football trade, but also many other lessons that equipped me for the rest of my life. Young players were not so cosseted as they are today. There was plenty of hard graft, a very strict disciplinary code and a need to respect your seniors and to do as you were told. I had already had those standards drummed into me when I was at home and this was more of the same.

It stood me in good stead for the remainder of my life. I have often been referred to as Goody Two Shoes and on one infamous occasion as Mary Poppins but I would much rather be known for my standards of behaviour than for being a wayward, disrespectful individual who was always in trouble with the authorities. I am not saying I have lived the life of a saint (no pun intended) but I think I learned very early in life when not to cross the line between having some fun and behaving badly.

I fell in love with professional football from the word go. I loved the atmosphere, even the smell of the dressing room. I loved the banter among the lads, the endless wind-ups and childish pranks. I loved the camaraderie and the feeling that you were part of a group of people who depended on each other through thick and thin.

Later in my career, I arrived at other crossroads that left me with more vital decisions to make. One of the biggest was when I announced I was to give up playing for England after the Euro 2000 tournament. Some friends thought I was mad. I was captain of my country, finding the net regularly and the all-time England scoring record of 49 goals held by Sir Bobby Charlton was by no means out of reach.

But I knew something had to give. My body was telling me it could not face the endless grind of playing season after season in the Premiership and then having to play through summer tournaments and major championship finals. Injuries had gradually started to take their toll and I felt sure that if I continued with that workload my Newcastle career would suffer. Added to that, I felt my family deserved more from me and, with another child on the way, it was good to be able to spend the summer months with them.

So it was farewell to England – another tough decision but one I took without any fear that I would live to regret it. There were hints in later years that an England recall could have been on the cards, notably when Sven-Goran Eriksson was the England coach, but I stuck rigidly to my original decision. I was definitely not for turning.

Only once did I change my mind over a major career decision. I was due to quit playing at the end of the 2004-05 season. But as the final curtain was within sight, I was playing particularly well, the goals were still flowing and people were banging on at me to give it another year. I gave in to the demands and the extra season gave me the chance to break the Newcastle scoring record, though that was never an influential factor in my decision to play on.

When it was eventually all over a year later, I limped across the finishing line having picked up a knee injury in a victory over arch-rivals Sunderland. It was not the ideal way to finish, with my leg strapped in a brace, but I felt I was leaving the game at the highest level. Throughout my career I was always certain that I would quit while I was still at the top.

I would hate to have slipped through the lower leagues and for people to say: 'That's Alan Shearer. What a good player he used to be.'

When people look back over my career I suppose I will be remembered mostly for my goals. I am pleased about that. Every single one of them has brought me pleasure from the moment I scored a hat-trick on my full debut for Southampton in 1988 right through to my final goal in my last game against Sunderland. That marvellous swishing sound as the ball rips into the back of the net has always been music to my ears.

Don't ask me where that ability to score goals came from. I reckon I was born with it. I was blessed with a natural gift to strike the ball powerfully and to get myself into the right scoring positions. And I have been dedicated enough to work on my game on the tactical and technical side.

Football has been good to me and I hope in some small way I have contributed to the greatest game in the world.

I was fortunate enough to bow out at my testimonial game in front of a full-house at St James' Park with my name ringing around the stadium. That moment will live with me forever. I was among my own people.

I can look back and say I have played for the Geordie fans wearing the famous black-and-white No 9 shirt. Life doesn't get much better than that. Regrets? Not a single one.

I WILL TELL YOU WHAT I GOT AT NEWCASTLE AND IT WAS PRICELESS… THE CHANCE TO WEAR THE BLACK AND WHITE NO 9 SHIRT, THE ADULATION OF THE MOST FANATICAL SUPPORTERS IN THE WORLD AND THE OPPORTUNITY TO BREAK A SCORING RECORD THAT HAD STOOD UNBLEMISHED FOR 50 YEARS. MONEY COULD NOT BUY THE PLEASURE AND PRIDE THAT BROUGHT INTO MY LIFE.

1 CHILDHOOD

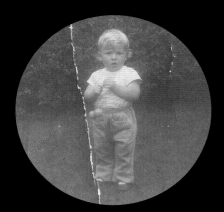

THEY WERE HUMBLE BEGINNINGS, NO DIFFERENT TO MANY THOUSANDS OF OTHER GEORDIE KIDS, BUT MY CHILDHOOD ON THE PARK AVENUE ESTATE IN GOSFORTH WAS EXCEPTIONAL IN MY EYES. IT WAS THERE THAT I LEARNED HOW TO KICK A FOOTBALL. OR RATHER I WAS MADE TO KICK ONE.

In those working-class households you didn't have much choice because the man of the house would waste no opportunity in taking his lad out into the back garden for a kick-about. My dad – also named Alan – was typical of the times. As soon as I could walk Dad threw a ball at my feet and gave me my first football lesson.

Now Dad would be the first to admit he was not out of the ordinary as a player. He loved the game with a passion and enjoyed nothing more than a game with his workmates. He was determined to pass on his enthusiasm to his only son and I was a willing learner.

Dad tells me I could always strike the ball well, even in those early days, and there were many broken windows in the house and the garden shed to vouch for that. Don't ask me where my ability came from. I must have been born with it but I didn't care too much about the origins of my skill. I just loved belting the ball as hard as I could towards imaginary goals.

It's strange now that I go through the same ritual with my lad Will. He loves nothing more than dragging me into the garden to kick a ball around for hours on end. There are no broken windows but I detect in him the same enjoyment I am certain I used to feel when I was that young.

Often I am asked whether I would allow Will to become a professional player. My answer is that if he wanted to, and had the right ability, I would encourage him to follow in my footsteps. Why should I stand in the way of my son wanting to do the greatest job in the world?

I am certain I used to drive my dad crazy with my non-stop demands to come out to play football with me. He worked as a sheet-metal worker and I guess he would be knackered when he arrived home from work – only to find me tugging at his sleeve to come out into the garden.

He never complained about it, and nor did he or my mum, Anne, when it came to kitting me out with a new pair of boots or the latest Newcastle United strip. Dad would drop all of his loose change into an empty whisky bottle and when there was enough cash he would take me to the local sports shop to buy yet another new pair of boots. When I was old enough to step into the outside world, or rather the patch of grass on the estate near our house, my football education took another step forward. Not only was I able to test my ability against the other kids – a lot of them much older and bigger than me – but also I sharpened up my goal-scoring. There was a pair of dark brown double doors adjoining the grass and they provided a perfect goal.

You had to lift the ball up and over a row of steps to score and that was an added test of skill. We learned to run fast there as well. The banging of the ball against those doors and the occasional shattering of glass as another window was destroyed had the residents of the nearby student flats chasing us away at high speed.

My initial experience of organised football came when I went to school, Grange First. It came in the form of six-a-side matches against other school teams on shortened pitches with small goals. I was a midfielder, not a striker, in those days, for no other reason than it meant I could get more involved in the games. I would take all the throw-ins, corners, free-kicks and generally tried to run the show. I am sure if it had been possible I would have taken corners and tried to get on the end of them to put the ball in the net. I was quick but not that quick!

As I moved on to Gosforth Central, the game became more organised and more serious with 11-a-side contests on full-size pitches. I was made team captain and that made me feel very proud. In one of my early games I ripped my knee open when I slid on to a piece of glass. It needed six stitches but I carried my injury like a badge of honour. It hurt like crazy but I limped around, pretending I was some professional recovering from a career-threatening injury.

I loved to score goals. I never grew tired of that fantastic, distinctive sound the ball made when it bulged the net. I was doing so well in school matches that one of the teachers, Mr Docker, suggested I should join the Wallsend Boys' Club side, with whom I enjoyed my first experience of proper training. Dad used to drive the 25-minute journey twice a week for training and for the Sunday games but he never saw it as a problem.

I LOVED TO SCORE GOALS. I NEVER GREW TIRED OF THAT FANTASTIC, DISTINCTIVE SOUND THE BALL MADE WHEN IT BULGED THE NET.

I think he recognised then that I was keen and had some ability and he wanted to allow me every chance to fulfil my potential. He was not averse to throwing the occasional financial incentive my way, either. I remember one game when we were winning 13-0 and I had failed to score. Dad yelled out to me: 'Smoky (that was my nickname because of my love for smoky bacon crisps), bet you a quid you can't score.' I found the net with each of my next three touches to complete my fastest ever hat-trick. Bribery works wonders at that age.

The touchlines at many of our Boys' Club games were filled with secretive-looking men who stood all alone watching the action intently. We discovered they were scouts from the professional clubs, running the rule over the local lads. There was an old saying in the north-east that if Newcastle wanted a new centre-forward all they had to do was whistle down a coal mine shaft and the new Jackie Milburn would appear.

Now that most of the pits are closed, the search for football talent is a bit more organised. I was lucky that I was spotted quite early on by a guy called Jack Hixon, a scout for Southampton, who made it known to my dad that he would like me to go to the south coast club for a trial. 'Ask him yourself,' was Dad's reply. 'He's old enough to make up his own mind.' It is true that my parents always encouraged me to stand on my own two feet, stand up for myself, speak my mind and develop my own personality. I am just the same now with my own kids, Will and his two older sisters, Chloe and Hollie. Though the world is a different and more dangerous place than when I was growing up, I try to give them their independence and freedom to go out and make decisions for themselves.

I was delighted to accept Jack Hixon's invitation to go for trials at Southampton, a well respected club in the top division of the Football League, and that began a friendship that is still strong today. Jack has almost become part of the family. I don't think there has been a week in my life when I haven't spoken to him at least a couple of times. He costs me a fortune in phone calls but it is worth it. Jack is a wise old so-and-so who offers advice only when I ask for it and is always there when I need him. Once when he was seriously ill in hospital, I was on England duty and got a message to say he might not make it. I dropped everything to be at his bedside and, I'm thankful to say, he pulled through.

I am afraid my schoolwork suffered as a result of my growing obsession with football. I would not recommend this to kids today. It is important to have a good education even if you think there is no other life for you but to be a footballer, a fashion model or a pop star. That is a message I am always drumming into my kids. I did just the opposite. It was football or nothing. Once when I was given a careers questionnaire at school I put 'dustbin man' in the space where it asked for career ambitions. Dad gave me a clip around the ear for that and made me change it to 'joiner'. But I think both he and I knew there was only one life for me.

I left school with just one qualification to my name – in English oral. You had to stand in front of the examiner and give a talk on your chosen subject. I prattled on about football for about a quarter of an hour and probably was given a pass for my cheek.

I went for trials at several clubs, including West Bromwich Albion, Manchester City and my beloved Newcastle United. It is part of Geordie folklore that I was made to play in goal when I went to Newcastle, but that is not strictly true. They asked if anyone fancied having a go between the sticks and, in an effort to show I was keen, I shot my hand up. I played in goal for about 20 minutes before someone else took over.

By this point most of my summer time was being taken up at Southampton Football Club. I would travel down in the school holidays with other lads from the north-east. We would get the National Express 'Clipper' coach down to London and then the train to Southampton. Most of the journey was spent larking around on what was a great adventure.

But it was serious stuff once we got to the football club. Playing against lads from all around the country was a real test. It was all very well being cock of the north-east but it was so much harder when you were up against outstanding youngsters from further afield.

There was a slight doubt at one stage whether I would be offered a Youth Training Scheme contract by Southampton and decision day was 3 April 1986, the date of my final trial match. I think it was the fear of being rejected that spurred me on that day and I scored five goals. Jack Hixon was there to watch me and one of the Saints coaching staff said to him: 'We'll be taking young Shearer on.'

'Mmm. I thought you might,' replied Jack, bristling with annoyance that there could be any doubts about it. I was on my way in the professional world and I couldn't wait to get started.

A regular supply of clean underpants and the occasional food parcel from my mum was my lifeline to home but generally speaking I was on my own – and that's just how I wanted it. I needed to stand on my own two feet and make my way in the big wide world as well as developing my football career.

I still reckon those early years in Southampton were the making of me. They gave me a feeling of independence that has stood me in good stead ever since. I became accustomed to making my own decisions and sometimes I had to learn from the mistakes I made. I discovered that the life of a professional footballer could be tough and competitive and that if you wanted to get on in the game you had to fight your own corner. They were character-building times and I look back on them with real affection.

This is where it all began for me as a budding footballer. Our back garden at Park Avenue was the setting for my regular kick-abouts with my dad. Even at this tender age when I was barely able to walk, he reckons I could strike the ball pretty well, and the better I got at it, the more Dad encouraged me.

This kind of support was worth its weight in gold. We were not particularly well-off but I never went short of anything when it came to football gear. Dad used to put all his loose change in an empty whisky bottle and when there was enough cash, he would use it to buy me a new Newcastle kit or a pair of boots.

Opposite: I was very fond of my food and this early shot of me on a family outing to the beach during a rare sunny day in Newcastle shows how upset I was when I dropped my sandwich in the sand. I am assured I was well behaved as a toddler, but still capable of the occasional tantrum.

I developed a passion for smoky bacon crisps when I was a bit older and some members of the family referred to me as Smoky, though I would like to think that was due to my blistering pace and powerful shooting.

I used to love going to school and this is an early portrait of me at Gosforth Central. My excellent attendance record was not because I was a great academic. It was more to do with me wanting to play football at break time and having a good laugh with my schoolmates.

Opposite: My first organised matches were at Grange Primary and I am the tiny figure squeezed in second from the right on the front row. Because I was born in August, I was one of the youngest and smallest boys in my year but that didn't stop me wanting to take all the free-kicks, throw-ins and corners.

I wanted to be involved in everything. I must have been a real pain in the backside at times but you couldn't knock my enthusiasm. I really was football crazy.

My first meeting with my earliest hero Kevin Keegan (opposite, top left) came when I won a competition in the local newspaper to attend a soccer skills school. I have to own up and admit I cheated because my mum filled in the entry form for me. That didn't matter. I was able to meet Kevin and show off my skills to him, though he obviously didn't see anything too exceptional back in those days.

It was enough just to have my picture taken with him and some of the other Newcastle players like Mick Martin (top right). I was an avid United fan and would regularly watch their home games from the Gallowgate End. I supported the team but I could never take my eyes off Keegan. He was such a charismatic person and an amazing player. Someone once described him as a Pied Piper character and that was pretty apt.

From what I can remember, he was brilliant with all the kids – not at all showy or big-time in the way he talked to us. I was pretty tongue-tied, but left him in no doubt that I was his biggest fan.

The Wallsend Boys Club was a breeding ground for many youngsters who went on to make the grade as professionals. They included the likes of Peter Beardsley, Steve Bruce, Michael Carrick, Steve Watson and Lee Clark. I managed to pick up quite a few medals in my time at the club and it was always the highlight of the year when one of the Newcastle players came along to the presentation evenings to hand out the prizes.

Barry Venison (below left) and Mick Tait (below right) did the honours on these two occasions. I was starting to shoot up in size as the picture with Mick shows and my fashion sense was developing, though I am not so sure about the drainpipe trousers.

I was captain at Gosforth Central when I won my first trophy for a tournament involving schools in the Newcastle area. On the pitch it was difficult to define my role. I was a midfielder-cum-striker-cum-defender.

I still had not got past that stage of wanting to be involved in everything, chasing the ball around like a headless chicken. No-one complained so I must have been doing all right. It was only when I started playing for Wallsend Boys and the Newcastle City Schools side that greater discipline came into my game and I moved up front to play as an out-and-out striker.

My first representative call-up was for the Newcastle City Schools under-13s. That's me on the right of the front row. The team was made up of the cream of youngsters from the region and it was a big breakthrough towards my ambition of becoming a professional footballer.

The games would attract a few scouts from leading clubs and I was fortunate that at one match in Benfield Park there was a guy called Jack Hixon patrolling the touchline. He liked what he saw in me and invited me for a trial at Southampton.

It was the start of a life-long friendship between Jack and myself and he has always been there to provide help and guidance. There was still a long way to go before I made it as a pro but those early steps were vital.

I had really settled into my striker's role by then and began to develop my appetite for scoring goals. I suppose I was a bit greedy when it came to poaching chances but, as I found out during my career, that is not a bad habit for a centre-forward.

At every opportunity I wanted to be kicking a ball around. In this picture there was a match in progress but still I couldn't resist getting in some shooting practice behind the goal. I didn't have to be told to work on my skills. It was something I just loved doing and I spent virtually every waking hour with a ball at my feet.

Opposite: What a proud moment it was for me when I played on St James' Park for the first time. The City Schools team reached the final of a seven-a-side tournament and we came away as the trophy winners. I'm on the right, clutching the silverware. My first time on the sacred turf was so exciting and I knew then that I wanted to play for United and become a hero.

Football didn't occupy all my time as a youngster – just 99 per cent of it! I used to love going on day trips from school, mainly because it meant missing lessons. I loved having a laugh with my mates, as we did on this expedition to Marsden Rock on the north-east coastline. We mucked about like most kids, but always knew when it was time to behave. I grew up being taught to respect my elders and I knew I would be in big trouble at home if I stepped out of line.

My love of food was so great I even scoffed someone else's while they were still eating it! This was another school trip to the coast. I was fortunate to grow up surrounded by some fantastic countryside and glorious beaches, and we made the most of them when the weather was good.

The boy was starting to develop into a man. I moved down to Southampton when I was only 15. I revelled in the freedom of living away from home after overcoming my initial homesickness.

Left: Showing off my physique and suntan in the garden of my first digs. If I ever find the person who gave me that haircut I will sue! **Above:** I had already started to put together an honours collection, with my England under-17 cap taking pride of place.

2 SAINT SHEARER

'STICK YOUR BUM OUT – JUST LIKE DALGLISH.' IT WAS HARDLY THE MOST TECHNICAL OR TACTICALLY ASTUTE PIECE OF FOOTBALL ADVICE I EVER RECEIVED, BUT IT WAS DELIVERED TO ME ON AN ALMOST DAILY BASIS BY THE SOUTHAMPTON MANAGER CHRIS NICHOLL.

Chris used to spend hour upon hour with me on the training ground or in the gym, working on my first touch and teaching me to receive the ball with my back to goal and hold off opposition defenders. He would throw and kick hundreds of balls to me at various heights and speeds to improve that vital control that modern strikers need.

The Saints boss was honest enough with me to point out that I did not have the same flair or natural ability as my contemporaries Matthew Le Tissier and Rodney Wallace. I was seen as a bit of a late developer who needed to polish up his technique. I had determination and a work ethic. I was quick, packed a powerful shot and had a willingness to spend however long it took to iron out the shortcomings in my game.

The one asset that Chris Nicholl immediately recognised was my anatomy: strong thighs, wide hips, a low centre of gravity – and a bigger than normal backside. Modern strikers spend so much time with their backs to goal, receiving the ball, holding off defenders and buying time for colleagues to link up in support. They need to be strong to withstand the battering they take from ruthless centre-halves and I was never lacking in that department. To be likened to the Liverpool legend Kenny Dalglish (later my manager at Blackburn and Newcastle) made me study him quite closely and realise that I had to use any advantage I could muster to gain that vital extra yard of space.

The England goalkeeper Tim Flowers, who became one of my best mates at Southampton, described me in a rather unflattering way when he first saw me at The Dell. 'The thing that first struck me about him,' said Tim, 'was that he had this bloody awful hairdo, parted at one side with a big quiff at the front. He also had these enormous, strong thighs. They looked like they were men's legs stuck on a kid's body.'

That kind of mocking humour and dressing room banter is typical of what goes on at all football clubs. You dare not let it get to you or you'd get more of it in bucket-loads. And you have to learn to give as good as you get. Personally I loved the humour and the tricks and pranks. It got me into trouble at times but I was just a young lad living away from home for the first time and free from the disciplines of family life. I was still 15 when I made the long journey to Southampton from Newcastle Central Station to step into the big world of professional football. There were a few tears from Mum and Dad as they waved me off but I was excited about what lay ahead of me.

Apart from the occasional weekend and the summer holidays back in Gosforth, Southampton was now my new base. I was a bit homesick at first but was fortunate enough to have fellow Geordies Barry Wilson, Tony Johnson, Neil Maddison and Adrian Ibbotson with me and initially we all made sure we were never lonely or stuck for something to do.

I stayed in digs just five minutes walk from The Dell and lived with a family called the Warehams, who guaranteed I was comfortable and well cared for. Regular parcels of underpants and socks were delivered from my mum to make sure I was clean as well! My first week's wage packet contained £27.50. Southampton also paid for my digs and gave all the trainees £20 a month for a bus pass. I didn't need mine because I could walk to work, so that was a nice little bonus.

I never had to drag myself out of bed in the mornings because I genuinely enjoyed getting to the ground and meeting up with the other lads. We would start at 8.45am and finish after 5pm. It wasn't all football. As well as training we had to make sure everything was spotless around the dressing room areas and that meant cleaning the boots of the whole playing staff, sweeping out the changing rooms, and disinfecting the medical area. It was a grind but we got on with it without complaint – well, most of the time.

It was all carried out under the watchful gaze of the youth team coach Dave Merrington, and he would not let anyone pull the wool over his eyes. He was tough but fair. Dave was a fellow Geordie and we got on very well but that didn't mean I was allowed any special privileges. If anything he was harder on me than the rest because he didn't want anyone to think I was getting preferential treatment.

One day Dave heard me complaining that it wasn't my turn to do a particular job and he laid into me. 'I'll tell you whose turn it is, bonny lad,' he

MY FIRST WEEK'S WAGE PACKET CONTAINED £27.50. SOUTHAMPTON ALSO PAID FOR MY DIGS AND GAVE ALL THE TRAINEES £20 A MONTH FOR A BUS PASS.

raged. 'Be here at seven o'clock in the morning and get the job done.' Another time I left the tap running in the boot room and flooded the medical room. That meant 50 laps running round the pitch in the freezing snow – not just me but the rest of the trainees as well.

That was Dave's way of telling us we were part of a team and we had to share our punishment as well as the praise. It was a team effort, but all of us were very independent and single-minded in our bid to get noticed and progress through the football ranks.

Obviously I was doing something right because, soon after my 17th birthday, Dave Merrington started pushing for me to get a first-team place. I had managed only a couple of outings for the reserves but Dave thought I was ready for the big step up, and after making two fleeting appearances from the substitutes' bench I finally got my first senior start. On 9 April 1988 I found myself in the squad for a home game against Arsenal and the word was out that Danny Wallace was struggling with an injury. I was having a pre-match meal at the Southampton Park hotel when Chris Nicholl came over to the table and said: 'Alan, you're in.'

The late call-up meant I didn't have a chance to get nervous, but it left me with some regrets because it didn't allow enough time for Mum and Dad to travel down from the north-east and share my big day. Nerves began to jangle as the kick-off approached, though, and I was shaking like a leaf when I ran out before the start.

Sometimes I think there is a force of destiny at work in our lives and everything is mapped out for us in advance. Whoever was writing my script that day must have had a very vivid imagination. Within five minutes I had scored with a header through Arsenal goalkeeper John Lukic's legs, then just after the half-hour I found the net with another nod. Soon after half-time the unthinkable, the virtually undreamable, happened when I pounced on a rebound from the crossbar to complete my hat-trick.

Talk about fiction. No-one could have made that up. I was protected from the press, who were waiting to speak to me after our 4-2 victory, because Chris Nicholl did not want me to be exposed to too much publicity so early

SOON AFTER HALF-TIME THE UNTHINKABLE, THE VIRTUALLY UNDREAMABLE, HAPPENED WHEN I POUNCED ON A REBOUND FROM THE CROSSBAR TO COMPLETE MY HAT-TRICK.

in my footballing life. His argument was that he didn't want me to get carried away with my own importance by believing my career had taken off when, in reality, it had barely begun. There was little chance of that. Next day I was in at work bright and early, cleaning the boots of those same players who had been my first-team colleagues the day before. The previous night, however, I had allowed myself a little celebration. I had started going out with a local girl called Lainya and she joined me and some friends for a few glasses of lager. Lainya was becoming more and more a part of my life. We had been introduced by Paul Masters, a fellow Southampton trainee, who was dating Lainya's sister Shona at the time.

Lainya and I got on straight away and started to see each other on a regular basis, going to the pub and the pictures, the same as any young courting couple. She earned more than me at the time in her job as a secretary so she was not after me for my money! Eventually I moved in with Lainya's mum and dad and by the time we were 18 we had bought our first house, a two-bedroomed semi.

With a mortgage to pay it wasn't long before I was glad to be offered a full-time professional contract. In fact, Chris Nicholl called me into his office a week after my hat-trick debut against Arsenal, though he omitted to tell me that Newcastle had been asking him if he would let me join them.

I don't think it would have mattered too much if had known there was an opportunity to go home. I was happy at Southampton, enjoying both my social and professional life, and felt I could make the right progress if I stayed put.

I felt like a millionaire when I put my name to a three-year contract worth £225 a week in my first year, £250 a week in my second and £300 a week in my third. Additionally I would be getting a signing-on fee of £18,000 spread over three years and I spent the first £6,000 of that on a B-registration Ford Escort.

There were no agents around to help young players in those days. I did all my own negotiations and I reckon I did a good job. Chris also promised me another pay rise when I was a first-team regular.

Just over a year later I went to see him again and my negotiating skills were not quite as impressive as I had believed. Chris sat stubbornly behind his desk and insisted I had done nothing to earn an increase. About two hours later when I was still banging on about a rise he thumped his fist on the desk and screamed at me to get out.

Lainya and I got married on 8 June 1991 at St James' Church in Southampton. We were both only 20 but realised even then that we wanted to spend the rest of our lives together. Footballers' wives don't always get a good time from the media and that is understandable, given the way some of them have behaved in recent times. I am glad to say that my wife is reserved and would run a mile at the sight of press photographers. She has had much to put up with, especially with me being away such a lot on international duty and overseas club trips, often when most families are on holiday enjoying the summer break.

I will tell you a little story about how understanding my wife could be. Just before we got married I returned from an England Under 21 tournament in Toulon and it was being hinted that I might get a call-up for the full England squad that was going on tour to Australia and New Zealand. It coincided perfectly with our wedding day.

Lainya and I discussed it and she was the one who insisted that I had no choice. It had to be football first and our wedding would have to wait. In the end I didn't get the call-up so our plans to get married went ahead. But I cannot think of many women who would have postponed the biggest day in her life so her husband could travel half way round the world to play football.

Lainya has got on with being a great wife and mum to our three kids, Chloe, Hollie and Will, without complaint. My family was one of the main reasons why I gave up playing international football following the Euro 2000 Championships. I felt I owed it to them to spend some quality time with them having been away from them for almost ten summers.

Two years into my first professional contract I got myself a new deal which took me up into the £1,000-a-week bracket, which meant that Lainya and I could afford some of the luxuries that had previously been denied us, including a new £140,000 four-bedroomed house. We bought that just before we were married.

Oddly enough, I was not able to establish myself as a regular goal-scorer for the Saints after my dream debut. I am sure some people thought I was just a flash in the pan, but I must have been doing reasonably well because I was getting regular first-team football and being well rewarded by the club.

But I made only two more starting appearances during my debut season. I suppose that was Chris Nicholl's way of reminding me that although I had made a stunning impact in my first game against Arsenal I still had an awful lot to learn as a striker and that's when I out in those extra hours on the training ground, improving every aspect of the game. For anyone who thought I had become an overnight sensation here was the proof that I was far from being the finished article. It was sometimes boring and repetitive but gradually my first touch improved until it became a habit to bring the ball under control with my back to goal from whatever angle it came to me.

I did not let it get me down because I realised that football is as much about hard graft as glory and while I grew a little bit impatient I never complained about having to work my shift in reserve games in front of a few hundred people.

During those early days I was very much in the shadows of my two striking contemporaries, Matt Le Tissier and Rod Wallace who came through the Saints youth system with me. They had both earned reputations as flair players while I was seen as a grinder and a grafter. I often used to joke with Matt that the reason he was so much more prolific than me as a goals scorer was because I did all the running for him.

There was no doubt that Matt was a very gifted individual but if I had one criticism of him it was that I never felt he truly realised his immense talent. He was a laid back person off the pitch and took that attitude with him onto the field. He did not seem to have the drive or ambition to push himself beyond the limits and was quite content to be the big fish in the little pond and spend the whole of his career at the Dell. But you had to respect his wishes and he was more than happy with his lot. That is all that mattered to him at the end of the day.

Matt was given licence to play where he liked and it was left to the likes of me or the other main target men Paul Rideout and Colin Clarke to put ourselves about and act as the suppliers of chances for Matt and Rod Wallace whose lightening pace allowed him to bomb past opposition defences. My job was unglamorous and hard work and it was no surprise that they were grabbing 20 goals a season and I was struggling to make double figures.

Eventually the goals started to flow during the 1991-92 season, when I hit 21 from 60 games in all competitions. I was getting some great help in those days from senior professionals like Mark Wright, Jimmy Case, Colin Clarke and our madcap goalkeeper John 'Budgie' Burridge.

Budgie has dined out for years on a story about a training ground incident when he had a right go at me – for not battering him. I was chasing a through ball and jumped over him as he threw himself at my feet. He went potty at me. 'Look son, when a 'keeper goes down at your feet, he expects you to clatter him,' he yelled.

A few years later he was playing for Falkirk in a friendly against the Saints and, sure enough, there was a goalmouth incident when Budgie had to dive in front of me. I followed through and caught him on top of his head. He needed three stitches in a wound and looked a right mess. But rather than slaughter me for causing the injury, he jumped to his feet, patted me on the head and said: 'Well done, son. I'm proud of you.' Mad as a hatter was Budgie.

The Saints boot boys are, left to right: Rod Wallace, Jamie Webb,
Phil Underhill, Neil Maddison, myself, Ray Wallace and Barrie Wilson.

During that 1991-92 season I started to attract the attention of the bigger clubs. I won my first full England cap, scoring on my debut in a 2-0 win over France in February, and the media were saying it was only a matter of time before Southampton would no longer satisfy my personal ambitions.

I never saw it like that. I was quite happy to continue learning my trade with the Saints, though I was intrigued to learn that I was being watched by other managers. Ian Branfoot had taken over from Chris Nicholl at that stage and one day my curiosity got the better of me. I knocked on Ian's door and asked if he would be good enough to let me know if there were any serious approaches for me from other clubs. Inevitably the press were linking me with Newcastle, while Manchester United were mentioned a lot and so were Blackburn Rovers, who had just embarked on a journey of success backed by their rich owner Jack Walker and under the management of Kenny Dalglish.

In the middle of the summer of 1992, I was having a quiet afternoon at home with Lainya, who was seven months pregnant at the time, when Ian Branfoot rang me. Southampton had accepted an offer from Blackburn, part of a deal worth £3.3 million that would also include David Speedie joining the Saints.

Still I was uncertain about what the future might bring. With my wife expecting, it was not a particularly good time to be uprooting ourselves and moving to the north of England. But I agreed to go and meet Rovers out of courtesy as much as anything else. The next stage of my career was calling me – but what did it have to offer?

Previous pages: We spent many hours larking about in the Southampton boot room, where one of our jobs was to clean the footwear of the professionals. It was a task to be taken seriously – if only because we would get a good tip from the seniors at Christmas if we did a good job. It was my task to take care of Mark Dennis's boots and he was always generous enough to give me £50, almost double my first weekly wage.

Dave Merrington, our youth team coach, taught us some real values and one of those was to do everything to the best of our ability. He was a tough taskmaster, but deep down he was a caring man who was always ready to promote our claims as we climbed the football ladder.

He used to take us to a shelter for the homeless and victims of drugs and alcohol to hammer home the message that there was a life away from football that was not as glamorous as ours.

I soon settled in Southampton, living in digs where everything was catered for. That was just as well because my cooking ability was very limited, to say the least. The best I could manage was a cup of tea and I am sad to say that's still the limit of my skills in the kitchen today.

My early career was a great adventure for me, an impression taken to new levels when we travelled to Sweden to play in a youth tournament. It was a marvellous feeling to be on foreign soil, representing not just your club but also your country, and we were fortunate enough to come home with the winners' trophy.

I think we were even allowed out for a spot of celebrating afterwards by Dave Merrington, but we never abused his trust in us. We knew if we strayed off the straight and narrow we would get no support from Dave and it would affect our chances of getting on in the game.

The Southampton youth team was full of attacking talent and I faced a lot of competition in the race for a first-team place. Matthew Le Tissier (back row, second left) and Rod Wallace (front row, second right) both made it to the senior team ahead of me, but when we eventually played together we all had something different to offer. Matt was one of the most skilful individuals I have ever seen but was laid back and never seemed to push himself to his limits. Still, he had a good career while remaining loyal to the Saints. Rod was lightning quick and together, with me playing the typical centre-forward role, we were quite a handful.

Right: Tim Flowers became one of my best mates when he signed for Southampton from Wolves. He also joined me at Blackburn, where he, Mike Newell and I used to travel to the Rovers training ground together from our homes near Southport. Our journeys were eventful, usually ending up in a row over something totally insignificant. We wound each other up non-stop and once we really upset Tim when we took his brand new Range Rover from the training ground and hid it. The three of us have remained good pals.

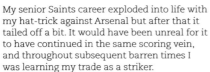

My senior Saints career exploded into life with my hat-trick against Arsenal but after that it tailed off a bit. It would have been unreal for it to have continued in the same scoring vein, and throughout subsequent barren times I was learning my trade as a striker.

I came to realise there was a lot more to being a centre-forward than putting the ball in the net. I learned about the need to hold the ball and link up with others, and to close down defenders when they had the ball. Back in those early days it was quite an achievement, also, to run around in those ridiculously tight shorts.

I built a reputation for back-chatting to officials over the course of my career, as seen in this picture of me sounding off to a referee or linesman (right). I never saw anything wrong with discussing an issue as long as I was not using foul language or being disrespectful.

I suppose that did give me a reputation as being a bit of a moaner but I should point out that I was never booked for dissent in more than 18 years in professional football.

This is me in a more composed mood. When I
started out I was mobile and willing to chase
anything that moved. I would never describe
myself as the greatest trainer in the world,
especially when it came to long-distance running.
But I was naturally fit and if you put a ball at my
feet, particularly with the goal in sight, I was as
fired up and energetic as anyone. When injuries
took their toll on me towards the end of my
career, gradually I had to adapt my game to use
my strength and experience.

3 **FEELING CHAMPION**

I DON'T KNOW HOW MUCH OF HIS PERSONAL FORTUNE JACK WALKER PLOUGHED INTO BLACKBURN ROVERS TO HELP HIM ACHIEVE HIS LIFELONG DREAM OF WINNING THE LEAGUE TITLE. WHATEVER THE AMOUNT, THE ONE THING THE CLUB'S OWNER COULD NOT BUY WAS THE TOGETHERNESS THAT BONDED THE SQUAD TOGETHER AS AN INDESTRUCTIBLE UNIT.

It was unique. You can have all the talent and skills you like but without that indefinable, magic ingredient it generally counts for nothing. We had it in barrel-loads at Rovers and the irony was that the rest of the football world claimed that Jack Walker had bought the title.

Sure, his investment in the team and the recruitment of Kenny Dalglish as manager gave us a fighting chance, but in the final analysis it was the lets-muck-in-together attitude that proved decisive. It was something I detected as soon as I went up to Lancashire to meet Kenny after Rovers had agreed a transfer fee with Southampton.

There was nothing grand about the club, certainly not in those early days, but it had a down-to-earth atmosphere that I found immediately appealing. In fact, there were parts of the club that were not really up to scratch. Before they built a new training ground complex, we used to use public pitches and an important part of Kenny's equipment was the spanner he carried in his tracksuit bottoms to bolt together the portable goalposts.

With Kenny at the helm, a feeling of genuine equality was generated. He was brought up the Liverpool way and that meant no-one was made to feel any more or less important than the rest.

I hit it off with my new manager from our first meeting. I went up with Lainya, who was pregnant with our first child, and he brought his wife Marina along for our initial talks. He seemed just as concerned about whether we would be comfortable with the move as a young family as he was about my ability to handle the football side of things. He wanted to know all about my upbringing and home life; as I was to find out later, he did that with all his new signings. He wanted no big-time Charlies in his dressing room. It was to be a team in every sense of the word, no matter how much each player cost.

From the moment I joined Blackburn, I was branded a greedy so-and-so who had spurned the chance to sign for Manchester United and Liverpool so

I could grab a big chunk of Jack Walker's loot. How wrong can you be? For a start, I never did have the opportunity to sign for United or Liverpool. Blackburn were the only club to agree a fee with Southampton, so that narrowed it down to a choice of one.

The financial terms offered to me by Blackburn were very generous but played only a minor part in my decision to sign for them. It was largely down to my gut instinct that Rovers could offer me the contentment that I was seeking, as well as the chance to win something. There was one more reason, and that was Ray Harford. Ray had been my coach when I had made my debut for the England Under-21 side and we had struck up a great relationship straight away. To have him as my coach on a daily basis was an opportunity I could not afford to miss.

Ray died from lung cancer in 2003 at the tragically early age of 58. I visited him at his home just before he passed away. What was said between us must remain private, but I needed to let him know how much he meant to me as a bloke and as a major influence on my career. The turn-out at his funeral some weeks later, with dignitaries from all over the football world, underlined how loved he was. I always maintained that I would want Ray as my coach if I ever moved into management, but sadly that was not meant to be.

Ray's knowledge and cheerful personality on the training ground and during match days was an integral part of that title-winning season. He and Kenny were magnificent partners, one dealing with the tactical stuff and the other with motivation and the mood in the dressing room.

Manchester United were our rivals on the run-in for the big prize and that brought the best – or should that be the worst? – out of their manager, Alex Ferguson. He played his little mind games as we got closer to the finishing line but Kenny refused to rise to his bait.

On one occasion Fergie said there was a danger we could do a Devon Loch, an oblique reference to the horse that fell on the run-in at a famous Grand National finish. 'Isn't that a stretch of water in Scotland?' Kenny responded in typical deadpan manner. When it came down to the final couple of matches, our manager came into his own. It was then that his decision to build a team

I WAS BRANDED A GREEDY SO-AND-SO WHO HAD SPURNED THE CHANCE TO SIGN FOR MANCHESTER UNITED AND LIVERPOOL SO I COULD GRAB A BIG CHUNK OF JACK WALKER'S LOOT.

in every sense of the word proved triumphant. There were no cliques or gigantic egos in that dressing room. If anyone stepped out of line he was quickly put in his place. Each member of the squad knew his job and was prepared to give blood and sweat for his team-mates.

Our form dipped at times but our spirit never wavered. I remember vividly one game against Aston Villa when our central defender Colin Hendry threw himself among the flying boots in a crowded six-yard box to prevent a certain goal. He risked getting his head kicked off but nothing got in the way of the Rovers' cause.

Towards the end of the campaign Kenny gave us one his most stirring team talks. 'It's all down to us now,' he said. 'We have come this far together so let's not throw it all away now. We are not top of the division through any fluke. We have been the best team in the League so let's go out now and confirm there is no-one better.'

There was a deep sense of irony that we clinched the title on the last day of the season at Anfield. We needed to beat Kenny's beloved Liverpool to seal it, no matter what Manchester United did at West Ham.

The Kop became Rovers fans that day because they could not stomach the thought of their hated rivals from along the M62 winning it. And of course, if they couldn't lift the trophy themselves, in their eyes there was no better man than Kenny to have it. The red-and-white of Liverpool merged with the blue-and-white of Rovers that day for a united celebration. We lost 2-1 at Anfield but Manchester United could only manage a draw at Upton Park.

So the title was ours and, amid emotional scenes, we were presented with the biggest prize in the domestic game. I could not help but feel a lump in my throat when I saw the trophy handed to Jack Walker. Here was the man who had devoted his life and a big slice of his hard-earned cash to bring the championship to his hometown club for the first time in 81 years. It was estimated by some that he had spent £60 million on Rovers, but if you had asked him I am sure he would have said it was worth every penny.

I was thrilled for Kenny Dalglish, too. I even felt this success meant as much to him, if not more, than all he had achieved at his previous clubs, Celtic and Liverpool. He had taken an unfashionable northern club from what used to be the Second Division and turned them into champions. Okay, he had the funds provided by Jack Walker at his disposal but, as we well know, football is littered with failed attempts to buy success. Kenny's achievement was all about his knack of bringing together an honest bunch of lads who refused to accept that second was good enough. The purists would argue that we were not the most attractive team in the world and that we had bought the title, but when the flak was flying we just closed ranks and became an even more tightly-knit unit. When the season finished we were just a single point clear of Manchester United and were the League's top scorers with 80 goals. So if anyone asks me whether we deserved to win it, I just point to the record books and tell them that history doesn't lie.

My championship medal now has pride of place among my personal collection. It is the only major club honour I have won but it carries with it the glorious memories of a season I will never forget. I played in all 42 League games that season, which made me the only ever-present. I scored 34 Premiership goals to win the Golden Boot award as the League's top scorer. I was voted PFA player of the year by my fellow professionals. I received further personal accolades from the Blackburn Rovers supporters' clubs.

So when people refer to me as a single-medal man, I feel I am well within my rights to tell them it was an achievement that carried with it so many other things to cherish. But I won't dwell on it. I know how much that season meant to every single member of the Blackburn squad. I doubt whether it will ever be repeated.

Even someone with Jack Walker's personal wealth would find it difficult to finance such a title challenge nowadays. We have moved into another financial era and I cannot see anyone breaking the monopoly held by the four 'superclubs', Manchester United, Chelsea, Arsenal and Liverpool.

Blackburn are the only club outside that elite group to have won the Premiership and they should feel very proud of that. And for those people who still harbour the idea that I went to Rovers only as a money-grabbing exercise, let me remind them of this: during four seasons at Ewood Park I scored 130 goals; I helped them win the title for the first time in 81 years; I became the first player to score more than 30 Premiership goals for three successive seasons; I won the Football Writers' Association player of the year award and the PFA player of the year award.

Rovers signed me for £3.3 million in a deal that included David Speedie going to Southampton. When they sold me to Newcastle my value had risen to £15.6 million. I think I proved I was good value for money!

Yet when I first went back to Blackburn as a Newcastle player I got a fair bit of booing and barracking. Some of it was good-natured but not all of it. It shows how fickle football fans can be, but I am sure that in the fullness of time the people of Blackburn will remember me with some affection. I know that's how I will remember them.

During the season after we won the title the first doubts started to enter my thoughts that Rovers might not be able to match my ambitions any more.

I don't mean that to sound selfish or self important but in a career you have to maximise your peak years and remain ambitious to win as many honours as possible. We had a disappointing European Champions League campaign and did not progress beyond the group stage. Kenny had asked to be moved upstairs to become director of football leaving Ray in charge of day-to-day management matters. Now that was not in any way a criticism of Ray but he was the first to admit he was not able to move the club forward as much as we would have wanted. At the back of my mind I started to wonder whether the good times were already over at Ewood Park.

It remains the unanswered question as to whether things would have been different if Kenny had stayed in charge. Who knows? But as far as I was concerned I missed Kenny's daily input on the training ground and I think Ray's contribution suffred as a result of his promotion to manager.

Our failure in Europe was matched by a similar dip in league form and we finished a disappointing seventh in the Premiership and that did not satisfy anyone who felt we should have been building on out title triumph. I was still able to score 31 league goals to win the Golden Boot award again but the nagging feeling grew that the really big team prizes were drifting out of reach. Offers had already started to come my way from other clubs – including the chance to move to Italy with Juventus indicating they were very keen to sign me. My advisor Tony Stephens was very well connected with the Serie A clubs having successfully negotiated his client David Platt's move to Italy.

We flew to Rome on a bit of a fact finding mission in the summer after we lifted the title and Tony was insistent I had a good look around the football scene and studied the culture and lifestyle there. At that time the Italian ahead of the Premiership in terms of glamour and finance and the temptation to move to adopt an exciting new way of life was great. Juventus were making it very clear that I figured as a big part of their future plans.

But something inside me was telling me it was not right. I did not feel comfortable with the idea of moving my young family to a foreign country. I knew the kids were too young to uproot from their home surrounding so I told Tony that when we got back home he should try to negotiate a new deal with Blackburn who were only too willing to offer me a new contract with a verbal promise from Jack Walker that I could leave whenever I felt unhappy with life at Ewood Park.

It was another of those key decisions that kept cropping up in my life. When I was younger I often said that I wouldn't mind playing in Italy at some stage of my career but when it came to it, my instincts told me it was not the right thing to do and my instincts never let me down.

There was a lot of pressure on me when I joined Blackburn from Southampton. Rovers had broken the British transfer record to sign me in a deal worth £3.6 million. That doesn't seem a lot by today's inflated standards but, believe me, I was expected to deliver. The price had nothing to do with me, of course, but the media have a way of raising the expectation levels and if you don't meet their targets, you can be labelled a failure immediately.

I managed to keep them quiet by scoring twice on my Rovers debut at Crystal Palace, but the rest of the season was a bit of a mixed bag. I ended it with a total of 22 goals from all competitions, which was not bad considering I missed half the campaign.

Strikers tend to hunt best in pairs and when Chris Sutton joined Rovers at the start of the 1994-95 season we developed a prolific partnership that was to reap huge dividends for the two of us and for Rovers. Soon we were dubbed the SAS (Shearer and Sutton) and wherever we went we scored goals.

I finished the season with 34 Premiership goals and Chris ended it with 15. Between us we played a big part in helping Blackburn to win the title. There were a lot of stories doing the rounds that Chris and I did not get on too well but that was nonsense.

I would not say we were the best of pals away from football but there was a mutual respect on the pitch and a healthy rivalry to see who could score the most goals. Chris was actually outscoring me at Christmas, but I had a good run later on.

We were similar in style – both strong-running, powerful in the air – and some might have suggested that we were too alike to hit it off as a pairing, but that did not stop us plundering some rich pickings. We were fortunate enough to have two great wingers in Stuart Ripley and Jason Wilcox to supply our ammunition. They could deliver crosses better than anyone in the Premiership.

This was the goal that many people thought won us the title. It was my header at the far post from a Graeme Le Saux cross that earned us a 1-0 win over Newcastle. It cemented our lead at the top of the table and though it was still possible for Manchester United to overtake us, this victory gave us a massive psychological lift.

Tim Flowers was incredible in our goal that night, producing at least four world-class saves. It was one of the best displays I have ever seen by a 'keeper – and just as good was Tim's performance in a television interview afterwards.

Alex Ferguson had been cranking up the pressure and wondering whether we were mentally tough enough to last the course. Tim delivered his response to the United manager in a live interview, ranting on for a good five minutes about how we had the bottle to win the title. It was memorable.

I felt as if I had the whole world in my hands the day I lifted the Premiership trophy at Anfield. I had waited a long time to win some silverware and, as it turned out, it was to be the only major club prize that came my way. That made it an even more special day in my life.

The population of Blackburn is around 140,000, so Rovers are very much a small-town club, but one of the townsfolk made it something very special. Jack Walker decided he wanted to put his beloved Blackburn on the map and he did it by spending money on the team.

The best move Jack made was to appoint Kenny Dalglish as manager with Ray Harford as coach. They built a team in every sense of the word. There was nothing complicated about the make-up of the squad.

We had defenders who could defend, midfield players who could tackle and pass the ball, two wingers who delivered deadly crosses and strikers who could score goals. Football can be quite a simple game if played properly. There were no square pegs in round holes. Everyone knew their job inside out and stuck to the script as written by Kenny and Ray.

Okay, it was an expensively assembled unit, but it did not involve the kind of massive investment we have seen in more recent times from the likes Chelsea, Manchester United, Arsenal and Liverpool. I doubt whether we will see a title-win like it again as long as the so-called Big Four dominate the scene.

I was proud to be voted Player of the Year by my fellow professionals on two occasions. There is no better compliment than being hailed by your peers. Here I am with the Young Player of the Year for 1995, Robbie Fowler, at the awards dinner.

Robbie was a talented striker for Liverpool and was revered around Anfield, where he was simply known as 'God'. He was a prolific goal-scorer at club level with a strike-rate of approximately a goal in every two games for the Merseysiders.

But he never quite hit the same levels as an international player. Often he was seen as the young pretender to my crown, but never managed to topple the old boy.

Kenny Dalglish managed to find a unique way of
separating me from Chris Sutton during the
Premiership title season. The judges couldn't split
us in the voting for the Carling player of the
month award in December and made it a joint
honour. Kenny settled the debate about who
would keep the trophy by sawing it in half.

Top: Finally I get my hands on a medal, though I thought I had lost it in the celebrations afterwards. It eventually turned up in our baby daughter's nappy bag!

Above: Chris Sutton and I complete a lap of honour with the Premiership trophy at Anfield, where the Liverpool fans stayed behind to share our day of glory. They were not just delighted that Kenny Dalglish had won it, but that we had kept it out of the hands of Manchester United.

Opposite: If anyone deserved to hold the trophy that day it was Jack Walker. He was a kind and generous man, but one who possessed a ruthless streak. You don't achieve what he did in his life without a touch of steel. I found that out when I tried to leave Rovers. He wanted me to stay and came very close to persuading me to give him another year.

Success on the field brought with it some extra rewards and I was fortunate enough to have a long-term association with Jaguar cars. This was the first I received as part of my sponsorship deal. I was lucky to have a good back-up management team, who took care of the commercial side of things, allowing me to concentrate on my football.

I always tried to give my sponsors value for money and was ready to spend a lot of time travelling to functions to endorse their products, provided it didn't cut across my training or playing schedules. It was necessary to find the right balance between activities on and off the field, and I think I did that. But football always had to come first, second and third.

4 PLAYING FOR ENGLAND

OWE AN AWFUL LOT TO GRAHAM TAYLOR. HE WAS MUCH MALIGNED AS AN ENGLAND MANAGER AND EVENTUALLY WAS HOUNDED OUT OF THE JOB HAVING BEEN CRUELLY DEPICTED AS 'THE TURNIP' BY ONE TABLOID NEWSPAPER. THAT WAS GROSSLY UNFAIR.

I suppose I am biased a little towards Graham because he gave me my first England cap in a friendly against France back in February 1992. I was able to mark my debut with my first international goal and it was one of those moments that will live with me forever. I can still play it over in my mind now . . . Nigel Clough's corner headed down by Mark Wright and me swivelling to hammer it into the net.

I went on to play 63 times for my country and score 30 goals but that first appearance will always remain a special one. Graham Taylor had enough faith to pick me when I was still a pretty raw rookie striker at Southampton and I'll always be grateful to him for that.

I rather suspect, though, that I got on his nerves more than once when I was pressing my claims to be included in his starting teams. There was one notable occasion in the build-up to the 1992 European Championships in Sweden when I might have pushed it a bit too far.

I had played only twice for the full England team and it was touch and go whether I would be in the squad. The waiting was killing me, so on the weekend before the announcement I went knocking on the manager's door in the hotel where we staying.

When Graham asked me what I wanted I told him straight: 'I would like to know whether I am going to be in your squad.'

'Why should I tell you?' he replied. 'Because I just asked you,' I responded.

Now Graham would have been well within in his rights to tell me to clear off and not be so insolent, but he was patient with me and said I would have to wait with everyone else to see who was in the squad. In the event, I was picked, but had limited opportunities in Sweden.

That was when Graham began to feel the heat of the media's criticism. When it was confined to the football it was fair enough but, more often, it was extremely personal and ridiculed him as a man. No-one deserved that, least of all Graham, who was a gentleman through and through, and refused to rise to the bait. Eventually he lost his job after failing to qualify for the 1994 World Cup finals in the United States.

A lot of people forget that Graham was without Stuart Pearce, Paul Gascoigne and myself at various stages of the qualifying campaign. I wonder how we would have fared if we had all been fit. I would suggest we would have qualified – and that would have changed the verdict on Graham Taylor as the England manager.

He was criticised often as a coach who relied too much on the long-ball game, and it was said that his tactics were not sufficiently refined to make his mark on the international scene. I can't go along with that. Sure, Graham liked his teams to get the ball forward quickly but it was never hit-and-hope stuff. As a striker I preferred it to be delivered early, either down the channels or into the penalty box. But, like any manager, he was judged on results.

By failing to qualify for the World Cup finals Graham was deemed to be a failure and so the Football Association decided he had to go.

It was a period of change within the England set-up. After the 1992 Euros, Gary Lineker retired just one short of equalling Bobby Charlton's all-time scoring record of 49 goals and I was being touted as Gary's natural replacement.

"How does it feel to be regarded as the new Gary Lineker," I was repeatedly asked by the media. I was at my diplomatic best in answering that one. "Of course it is very flattering to be compared to such a great striker," I responded. "But I would rather be recognised in my own right than be the new Gary Lineker."

Of course Gary and I were totally different players. He relied on his speed and stealth around the penalty box and he was master goal poacher. My game was more about power and penetration. The one thing we did share was an insatiable appetite to score goals – from whatever range and angle, and as long as the ball ended up in the back of the net.

It is a pity Gary and I did not have more opportunities to develop a partnership for England our respective strengths would have complemented each other rather nicely. But his international career was drawing to a close just as mine was taking off. Eventually we had to settle for sharing a studio as colleagues working for the BBC.

IN THE BUILD-UP TO EURO '96 I WENT THROUGH THE WORST GOAL FAMINE OF MY CAREER. IT LASTED 12 MATCHES AND 21 MONTHS

Graham was replaced by Terry Venables, a man who had earned a glowing reputation for his tactical and coaching expertise and who was popular among many sections of the media.

His primary task was to guide us to victory in Euro '96. I was a big fan of Terry as a coach. He reminded me in some respects of Ray Harford, for instance in the way he mixed so well with the players and made training so enjoyable.

Terry's support for his players was indestructible. That was very evident during our trip to the Far East before the Euro '96 finals. There was a massive media outcry when some of the players decided to let their hair down after the game in Hong Kong. Most of the squad went out for a drink and ended up at the China Jump Club where the infamous "Dentist Chair" incident took place.

You were strapped into the chair while various drinks were poured down your neck at a rapid rate. Mr "Goody Two Shoes" Shearer was not present for the real fun and games because I had to attend a promotion with my kit suppliers Umbro so I avoided being caught in the pictures that were splashed all over the English newspapers next day.

Further bad publicity was waiting for us after the flight home when a couple of television sets were damaged. We all held our hands up and accepted collective responsibility while the Press claimed we were all a national disgrace and should be barred from representing our country.

I would never condone vandalism but we shouldered the blame and had a whip round to cover the damage. Through it all Terry's support for the lads was unwavering and not once did he slag off any players publicly. He was also clever enough to use it to our advantage by bringing an even closer harmony to the group while the tabloids were howling at the door.

As is the case with Graham Taylor, I owe Terry a big debt of gratitude. In the build-up to Euro '96 I went through the worst goal famine of my career. It lasted 12 matches and 21 months and I started to wonder whether I would ever score for England again.

All the matches before the championship finals were friendlies because we qualified automatically as the host nation. Terry was under enormous

I WAS GIVEN THE ARMBAND AHEAD OF TONY ADAMS, STUART PEARCE, GARETH SOUTHGATE AND DAVID SEAMAN, AND THAT MADE IT EVEN MORE SPECIAL.

pressure to drop me but he refused. My repeated answer to the press questions about my lack of goals was: 'Don't worry. When the finals start and it really counts my goal touch will return.'

I was sticking my neck on the block there because, of course, I could not guarantee I would start scoring again. But what the media did not know was that Terry had taken me to one side and assured me that Teddy Sheringham and I would be the strikers who started for England when Euro '96 began. That was a massive relief for two reasons. Firstly, I did not have to worry about where my next goal was coming from, though obviously no striker wants to endure such a bleak spell. Secondly, I was delighted that Teddy would be playing alongside me. He was such a clever player and my favourite strike partner. He was not blessed with great pace but he thought a second or two ahead of anyone else.

He knew exactly when to pick his pass and was always unselfish enough to play a colleague in for a scoring chance rather than go it alone. He seemed to get as much pleasure out of creating opportunities as he did from scoring himself.

There was one goal during Euro '96 that summed up our partnership. It came in the 4-1 win over Holland that was arguably the best team performance I have seen from an England side. Teddy had already grabbed a couple of goals for himself and I had one from the penalty spot.

A scintillating passing move culminated in Gazza slipping the ball to Teddy on the edge of the box. Rather than go for goal and complete his hat-trick, he noticed I was in a slightly better position and slid me in to score with a shot that went in off the post. That was Teddy – always willing to sacrifice a slice of personal glory for the good of the team.

Unfortunately, our bid to lift the trophy ended when we were beaten by Germany in a penalty shoot-out in the semi-final. It was a cruel way to go out and Gareth Southgate was inconsolable after missing the vital spot-kick that cost us a place in the final.

But we did not attach any blame to Gareth. We shared the responsibility for the defeat as a squad and no-one was pointing any accusing fingers. We knew we were as good as any team in the tournament and I finished as the top scorer with five goals, but that was a small consolation.

We said goodbye to Terry Venables at the end of Euro '96. He felt that upcoming court cases in which he was involved would prove too much of a distraction to do his job properly. That was a great shame, in my view, because we were losing a coach of outstanding ability for reasons that had nothing to do with football.

My third England manager was Glenn Hoddle. This is all sounding rather sycophantic, but I had plenty of reasons to be thankful to him as well. Glenn bestowed on me the honour of being captain of my country. He called me into his room at the Burnham Beeches hotel, where we had gathered for a World Cup qualifier against Moldova, to ask me whether I fancied the skipper's role. He had hardly finished the sentence when I answered: 'Yes, of course I do.' I was given the armband ahead of Tony Adams, Stuart Pearce, Gareth Southgate and David Seaman, and that made it even more special.

At first I was handed the job for three games to see how I coped. Fortunately, I did well enough and continued scoring enough goals to prove the extra responsibility did not affect me. To follow in the footsteps of such great leaders as Billy Wright, Bobby Moore and Bryan Robson was truly spine-tingling

Leading out the team in Moldova was memorable enough, but when I walked out in front of the England side for the match against Poland at Wembley, with a massive crowd that included Lainya and my mum and dad, the pride was powerful enough to almost burst my shirt wide open.

I tried to be a captain who led by example rather than one who shouted and screamed and waved his fist at his team-mates. I think I earned the respect of my colleagues, to a large extent, by not changing my personality and just being myself.

Qualification for the 1998 World Cup finals was achieved eventually with a goalless draw against Italy in Rome. At the time I was thousands of miles away in Barbados, soaking up the sun and recovering from an ankle injury I had suffered against Chelsea in a pre-season friendly at Goodison Park. My dad gave me a running commentary down the phone line and once our place in the finals was secure I was determined I would be fit for the showpiece occasion in France.

I made it and expectations were running high when we kicked off our campaign with a 2-0 win over Tunisia. That made our progress into the second round so much easier and enabled us to witness the arrival on the international scene of a remarkable young man called Michael Owen.

He scored an astonishing goal against Argentina in the second round and, as he has since admitted many times, it changed his life beyond all recognition. We should have beaten the Argentinians that day, even after David Beckham was sent off for flicking his leg at Diego Simeone.

Sol Campbell had a goal disallowed when I was alleged to have fouled their goalkeeper with the scores still level in extra time. I swear to this day that Sol's strike should have been allowed. In the end we went out on penalties again, and another tournament that had started with so much hope finished with the sour taste of failure. One of my main memories of that defeat against Argentina was to study the extreme emotions of David Beckham and Michael Owen. On the coach pulling away from the stadium David sat silently with his head bowed, wrongly blaming himself for our exit. Little did he know that he was to return home to be greeted as Public Enemy No 1, with effigies of him being hung from lamp-posts and his picture used at the centre of a dartboard by one tabloid.

Michael was chatting excitedly on his mobile. He was as sick as anyone that we had lost, but knew the impact he had made on the world's biggest stage and realised that a new life was opening up ahead of him.

I know David and Michael as well as most because we shared the same management company and agent, Tony Stephens. They are entirely different personalities. Michael prefers to live his life out of the public eye in the safe surrounds of his family, while David has become a celebrity outside the football world, largely because of the fame enjoyed with his wife Victoria.

My life is similar to Michael's, but I would not dare to begrudge David his own lifestyle. He has coped with the intrusion exceptionally well and still managed to be one of the outstanding internationals of his era.

Michael has been affected so much by injuries that you start to wonder how much more he could have achieved. But I know from working with him at Newcastle and for England that he is a determined character who will make a very big contribution to club and international football in the years ahead.

Like Terry Venables, Glenn Hoddle was to depart the England hot seat for non-football reasons. He was hounded out for talking about religious views that offended some sections of the media. It was another ridiculous end to an England manager's reign, but it opened the door for Kevin Keegan to take over.

Kevin brought a real sense of enjoyment to the international scene. He had been my idol since I was a young boy. I watched him from the Gallowgate End at St James' Park and dreamed of emulating him one day. I was a ball-boy on the day he played his last match for Newcastle. I watched in awe as a helicopter lifted him away from the pitch at the final whistle and shed a small tear as he dropped his No 7 shirt out of the sky.

To play for Kevin as his England captain was a real joy. He was very much one of the lads, though some claimed he was too close to the players. I didn't share that view and all the stories about him organising big gambling sessions were completely wrong.

It was fun to play in that England team, though soon after he took over I began to have my first doubts about whether to continue my international career. I was starting to feel the strain of playing non-stop season after season, summer after summer, with hardly a break in between. I had suffered quite a few serious injuries over the course of my career and my body was starting to tell me it needed a rest somewhere along the line. I also felt I owed it to Newcastle to offer the remaining years of my career in top physical condition. In addition, the needs of my young family were becoming more of a priority and I wanted to spend more time with them during the close-seasons. So something had to give.

It was with a heavy heart that I decided to announce my retirement from international football. I said I would quit after Euro 2000, in which I hoped I could lead us to victory in my last game in an England shirt.

Sadly, that was not to be. We went out in the qualifying group after losing our final game 3-2 against Romania. Afterwards I sat on my own in the dressing room in Charleroi when all the other players had left. I wanted a few moments to reflect on my career as an England player.

There was the regret, of course, that we had failed to lift a major trophy. That is a mystery that remains to this day. Since England won the World Cup in 1966 we have reached the semi-finals of only two major tournaments.

We have earned the reputation of being quarter-final bottlers. That's a bit harsh, but I can understand why the accusation is levelled at us.

Subsequent failures in the World Cups of 2002 and 2006, and in Euro 2004, have hardened the opinion that we do not have the talent to test the top nations. Yet I think the talent is there. If you look at the squad that went to the World Cup finals in Germany in 2006, there is a not a single country that would not have swapped at least half a dozen English players for their own.

Rio Ferdinand, John Terry, Steven Gerrard, Frank Lampard, Michael Owen and Wayne Rooney would have walked into any other team in the finals. So why did we not perform as a unit? That's the million dollar question no-one seems to be able to answer.

We relied on a foreign manager, Sven-Goran Eriksson, to lead us into those campaigns after 2000. I had nothing against him as a bloke but I said at the time of his appointment that the job should have gone to an Englishman. It is a sad indictment of our game that we should have to rely on an outsider to shape the fortunes of the national team.

Exactly where the answer lies to England's failure to produce a championship-winning team remains a conundrum, and we need to scrutinise the sport from top to bottom. If I had the solution I would be straight on the phone to the England manager.

The under-21 team was a great stepping stone towards the full England squad. I scored on my debut against the Republic of Ireland and went on to grab a total of 13 from 11 appearances at this level.

That brought me into the international spotlight and England boss Graham Taylor kept a regular watch on my progress before picking me for his side. The under-21s also gave me an introduction to Ray Harford, the coach who was to have a profound impact on my career.

I went to an under-21 tournament in Toulon, France, where Ray was in charge of the side. We won the trophy and I came home with four goals from seven matches, as well as the Player of the Tournament award. More importantly, I benefited immensely from Ray's coaching and I reckon those couple of weeks working with him sowed the seeds of my move to Blackburn.

Above: My Southampton team-mates Jeff Kenna (centre) and Rod Wallace (right) also figured in that Republic of Ireland game, so it was a proud day for the club.

This was a moment that will never be erased from my memory – my first England senior goal in a friendly against France at Wembley. I struck the ball cleanly and powerfully and it simply flew into the net after Mark Wright had headed down Nigel Clough's corner. It is difficult to put your feelings into words at a time like this. To receive the acclaim of a full house at Wembley and the congratulations of your team-mates is beyond description.

It was the start of a scoring run for England that brought me 30 goals from 63 appearances. They reckon if you score a goal every other game at any level you are doing a good job, so I will let that particular statistic speak for itself.

I seemed to take the international game in my stride – just as I did my initial breakthrough into the Southampton side. I never allowed the occasion to get the better of me. There were nerves, of course. I would not have been human if I didn't suffer butterflies in the stomach before big games, but I always felt relaxed once the action started.

Our 4-1 victory over Holland at Wembley in Euro '96 was probably the best England team display I was ever involved in. I opened the scoring from the penalty spot, placing my shot well out of the reach of Edwin van der Sar. The level of that performance made everyone start to think we were capable of winning the tournament and it was easy to feel optimistic.

The Dutch couldn't live with us that day and the quality of our performance was underlined by our fourth and my second goal, which rounded off a scintillating build-up involving Paul Gascoigne and Teddy Sheringham. The win in our final group game took us through to meet Spain in the quarter-finals and we really started to fancy our chances.

Euro '96 was played in a real carnival atmosphere.
It was one of those summers when the sun never
seemed to stop shining and there was a smile
on the face of the whole nation as football
came home. There are few more exciting venues
than Wembley, particularly with a full house,
and the place was really rocking whenever we
took the field.

The tune of the moment was 'Three Lions', with
lyrics by the comedians David Baddiel and Frank
Skinner, and everywhere you went people seemed
to be singing it. Even the players sang a rousing
chorus on the team bus to and from games.

We read a lot in the papers about how England-
mania was gripping the nation but I realised how
great it was only when I left the team hotel to nip
into Burnham for a haircut after the Holland
game. The flag of St George was flying out of every
window, car horns and radios were at full volume
and people were singing and dancing in the street.
And that wasn't even a match day. If only we
could have rewarded the fans by winning the
trophy. What a party that would have been.

Arguably this was the most important England goal I ever scored. It came in our opening group game against Switzerland in Euro '96. I had more or less put my international future on the line by promising to score goals in the finals after going 21 months and 12 matches without finding the net for my country.

There were calls in the media for me to be axed before the tournament began but I kept telling people it would all come right when the real thing started. All the games in the build-up had been friendly internationals and I knew I had to deliver when Euro '96 began or I would face the chop for sure.

The first game was only 20 minutes old when my chance came. Paul Ince found me with a great pass and I smashed it into the net. I think I put 21 months of frustration into that shot. I rather overdid the celebrations, but I think I was allowed to go a bit over the top in the circumstances.

Overleaf: When I gave us the lead against Germany in the semi-finals of Euro '96, we felt we were going all the way and would lift the trophy. But you can never write the Germans off so easily and when they equalised it developed into a really tense occasion between two football nations who have been locked in many similar contests.

The golden-goal rule was in use, meaning that the scorer of the first goal in extra time would go through. Darren Anderton hit the post for us and Gazza was only a inch away from converting my cross as the minutes ticked away.

In the end we lost it on penalties. Gareth Southgate missed his spot-kick and out we went. This was a crushing disappointment and poor Gareth was inconsolable. It was a desperate way to be eliminated but I don't believe luck played a part in it. Everyone knew this was the way the game would be settled if the semi-final was level after extra time.

Leading out England for the first time was another of those emotional occasions that will live forever in my memory. It was a World Cup qualifier in Moldova and I managed to score in a 3-0 victory.

My reward at the end was a sloppy kiss from Paul Gascoigne, one of the other scorers. Gazza was unique. He was an incredible talent but a real one-off personality.

I was lucky enough to play alongside a lot of good strikers, but if you pushed me I would have to name Teddy Sheringham (left) and Les Ferdinand as the best of the bunch. Teddy partnered me many times for England and Les was my fellow striker when I joined Newcastle.

They were completely different in style. Teddy was not the quickest by any means, but could think a yard faster than most players. He could spot openings and was great at playing the early pass with exactly the right weight. Sometimes I thought he enjoyed creating goals as much as scoring them, but he did also grab a fair share for himself. He was in fantastic physical shape and was still playing Premiership football at the age of 40. He is also the oldest player to score in the Premiership and that is a wonderful tribute to the way he took care of himself.

Les was big and brave, tremendous in the air but skilful on the ground as well. He was the perfect build for a striker and used his physique to great effect. He was also unselfish, like Teddy, and could pull defences around, leaving space for his partners to exploit. When I joined Newcastle he was the occupant of the No 9 shirt and I made it clear to Kevin Keegan that I would like it. I knew the historical significance of that shirt and wanted to follow in the steps of all the greats who had worn it. Les handed it over and I learned later that he was not too happy about it. But he never mentioned it at the time and it never got in the way of our enduring friendship.

Above: This is a rare sight – an England captain holding up an international trophy. The occasion was Le Tournoi, which was a tournament contested by ourselves, Italy, France and Brazil in 1997 as a trial run for the World Cup finals a year later. We lost to Brazil but beat France and Italy to finish top of the four-team table and win the trophy. I became the only England skipper to lead a senior team to a tournament victory on foreign soil. It might have been only a minor prize but it put everyone in great spirits for France '98. If only...

Right: Going in where it hurts. No centre-forward worth his salt would hesitate to risk a punch in the head if there was the chance of a goal in the offing, especially if he was playing for his country.

When the World Cup finals began in 1998 our first game was against Tunisia. It was a testing game in very hot conditions in Marseille, but we got off to a flying start when I scored with this header in the first half. There is no better way to kick off a tournament than to get off the mark early on and the mood in the England camp was sky high.

Above: Sometimes a striker has to perform contortions in the quest for a goal.

Opposite: This became a familiar sight over the years. The raised-arm salute was my trademark celebration and here I am reacting to my opening goal against Tunisia at the World Cup. I don't know how it started but it became such a feature of my game that I prolonged it right to the end of my career. I was never one for going too mad when I scored – probably because it was waste of energy. Certainly you never saw me going in for those triple somersaults and back flips that some players performed. My poor old back would never have stood up to that.

Previous pages: The England line-up for one of the most talked about games of my career – the World Cup clash against Argentina in St Etienne in 1998. Back row, left to right: Michael Owen, Paul Ince, Darren Anderton, Sol Campbell, David Seaman and Tony Adams. Front row: David Beckham, Gary Neville, Graeme Le Saux, Paul Scholes and myself.

There were so many sub-plots to this dramatic encounter. We saw the emergence of the young Michael Owen with his dazzling solo goal; David Beckham became Public Enemy No 1 after being sent off; we lost the penalty shoot-out 4-3 after holding the opposition to a 2-2 draw for more than half the game. In the end we blew a great chance of going through with an outstanding team.

Left: This sequence shows my goal from the penalty spot during the 90 minutes against Argentina and my celebrations with Michael Owen and David Beckham. I also put away my spot-kick during the shoot-out.

Taking penalties was never a problem for me. It was a question of keeping my nerve, making a decision where I was going to put it and not changing my mind. After that I aimed to make sure I made good contact and tried to direct it out of the 'keeper's reach. Simple stuff. It sounds easy but it's amazing how many times the 'keeper wins the battle of nerves when really he should stand no chance against a player with a free shot from 12 yards. I always insisted on taking penalties for my club teams and I reckon my record stood up alongside anyone's.

Right: The feeling of dejection after we had been beaten by Argentina was obvious. It was another lost opportunity to make a big statement on the world stage. I don't believe our opponents were any better than us. They were just more efficient at taking penalties. To those who think it is a cruel and unfair way to decide such a big game I would suggest no-one has come up with a better solution yet. Until they do we have got to become more accomplished at scoring from the spot.

Above left: Bobby Robson was the guest of honour and was introduced to the two teams before the Euro 2000 qualifier against Luxembourg at Wembley. He is a well-loved figure in the English game – deservedly so. Our paths were to cross again at club level. **Above right:** Liverpool pair Robbie Fowler and Steve McManaman join in my hat-trick celebrations.

Opposite: Two views of my second goal in the 6-0 win over Luxembourg, which featured my only hat-trick in an England shirt. Critics said it was only against Luxembourg, as if we were expected to roll such teams over and get a bagful of goals. It doesn't work out like that, I'm afraid. It has become a cliché but there are not any easy games at international level any more.

The smaller nations have learned to organise themselves and have become very difficult to break down. When a team sets out to defend and rarely ventures into the opposition half, it takes a lot of patience to get behind them. England have found out in recent years that there are no whipping boys in international football.

I decided to hang up my England No 9 shirt for good in the run-up to the Euro 2000 finals. It was not an easy one to make. I consulted the people in the game whose opinions I trusted most, such as Kenny Dalglish and Kevin Keegan, and my close family. Some agreed with me and some didn't, but as usual I made up my own mind and once it was made up I stuck to it. Some people thought I was mad to turn my back on my England career. They argued that I had years of international football left in me and, if I stayed fit, I could go on to beat Bobby Charlton's England record of 49 goals.

Fitness was the key factor. My body had taken a pounding during my career and I was starting to feel the strain. Rest was becoming as important to me as working out on the training ground. Now I decided that the only way I was going to start every new season fit and well was to curtail my international appearances and spend my summers having a good rest. I had been involved in close-season tours and tournaments for eight years and it was time to spend some quality time with my wife and children.

But while that door closed, I was able to open a new phase of my service to Newcastle and I gave a press conference (above right) to explain why I was willing to devote the rest of my career to my club. I made it my personal crusade to win something for Newcastle. It didn't convert into trophies and medals, but it was satisfying to know I had done everything I could do to bring home some silverware.

I gave it everything to try to ensure my England career finished on a high note, but the big prize again proved beyond our reach at Euro 2000. As usual it started encouragingly enough with victories over Portugal and Germany, but it all went wrong when we lost to Romania 2-3, despite leading at half-time. Our participation in the finals was over and so was my international career.

I managed to equalise from the spot against Romania, but although Michael Owen gave us the lead soon afterwards, we were pegged back and went out of Euro 2000 in demoralisingly disappointing circumstances.

A final handshake (opposite), but the end came without the blaze of glory I was hoping for. There were no tears, by the way, despite appearances in the picture (above right). My gesture was merely one of despair at the end of another major championship without success after we had been eliminated from Euro 2000 by Romania. In the dressing room afterwards I did stay behind when everyone else had gone and reflected on what had been a great international career personally, but a frustrating one for the various England teams I had played in. But there was not too much dwelling on the past. I still had a club future to look forward to.

There was no going back, either. There were a few attempts to persuade me to don an England shirt again, notably when Sven-Goran Eriksson was manager, and it was flattering to know he thought I was still worth a place in his team. But my time had come and gone. Probably I could still have done a job for England but only at the expense of my club form. I had 63 caps and 30 goals, and that record had a nice feel to it. I was happy to stick on that.

5 THE GLORY OF
THE PREMIERSHIP

WHEN THE PREMIERSHIP WAS FORMED IN 1992, A REMARKABLE REVOLUTION TOOK PLACE IN ENGLISH FOOTBALL. SUDDENLY THE GAME GAINED A NEW IMPETUS AND A FRESH OUTLOOK. THE REST OF THE WORLD SAT UP AND TOOK NOTICE AND SOON THE STARS OF THE GLOBAL GAME BEGAN TO BE ATTRACTED TO THIS COUNTRY.

Of course, a lot of the interest was generated by the extra money that was now on offer from sponsorships and television deals. In my opinion the millions have generally been well invested and we now have the best league in the world. We have the top players, some outstanding managers, the best stadia, the biggest crowds and a level of excitement, commitment and passion that no other football nation can match.

Of course, we have the on-going argument that too many imported players have helped to stifle the development of English talent, with a detrimental effect on our national team. I can only go along with that view to a point. I am all in favour of the cream of the world's footballers arriving at these shores. But I do mean the cream – players like Thierry Henry, Dennis Bergkamp, Eric Cantona and the rest who have lit up our national sport. Where I disagree with the influx of foreigners is when clubs bring in overseas players who are no better, and in many cases, a whole load worse than the youngsters who are trying to work their way through the clubs' junior ranks.

But here we have a Catch-22 situation. A manager is paid to get results – quickly. Unless he has an unbelievably tolerant chairman, there is no time to let his home-grown kids develop. So the quick-fix solution is to nip over to the Continent or further afield and sign ready-made players from foreign clubs for relatively cheap fees.

That's why the game is clogged up with so many ordinary imports who are standing in the way of English lads. I know if our boys are good enough they will emerge and stake their claims with the top clubs, but it is getting more and more difficult.

Similarly the big Premiership clubs are likely to 'go foreign' rather than buy British from the lower leagues because the fees can be so much more reasonable. That halts the trickle-down effect of keeping the money in this country and helping the less well-off clubs in the lower divisions to stay afloat.

It is a difficult problem to solve. Limiting the number of foreign players per club has been suggested but that falls foul of the complicated European employment rules and I understand new laws would have to be passed.

Another problem with rising transfer fees and escalating players' wages is that all the power can be concentrated into the hands of a very small collection of clubs. The record books support this because only four clubs have won the Premiership title – Chelsea, Manchester United, Arsenal and Blackburn Rovers.

Blackburn broke the mould in 1994-95 because we had the investment of Jack Walker to help the cause, but it was nowhere near the mega-millions that are being pumped into the Premiership today. The influx of foreign owners – notably Chelsea's Russian billionaire benefactor Roman Abramovich – has isolated the top four clubs even more and it would take a brave man to tip anyone outside the elite group of Chelsea, Manchester United, Arsenal and Liverpool to become champions.

It has created another Catch-22 situation. The top clubs get the biggest crowds, generate the largest income from gate receipts and sponsors and therefore attract the best players. Their success is not guaranteed because money cannot always buy achievement, but certainly it gives them a head start on the rest. The challenge for those clubs just below the top four is to break the monopoly and that is easier said than done. It will take some astute transfer dealing and expert management to climb aboard the title-challenging bandwagon. For most clubs the priority is merely to stay in the Premiership and stake a claim to some of the riches that are up for grabs.

The other anti-Premiership argument is that it has priced the ordinary supporter out of a game that has now become the plaything of the rich and famous. As someone whose family grew up watching our heroes from the Gallowgate End of St James' Park, I can appreciate the fact that football is no longer a working man's sport. That's why I have been so pleased to see that some clubs have begun to peg and, in a few cases, reduce, admission prices in a bid to reverse the slight but worrying trend of falling attendances.

Players' wages have continued to climb and there have been calls for salary caps to be introduced in line with some of the American sports, but I would never begrudge a player earning the going rate in what is a very lucrative market. I would say that, wouldn't I, having been part of the pay boom that accompanied the introduction of the Premiership? But footballers are part of the entertainment business and are rewarded accordingly. If they were not giving value for money I am sure the fans would stay away in vast numbers, and the television companies would pull the plug and withdraw their cash.

Now that I have retired, I find the entertainment value of the Premiership is as high as ever. I would defy anyone to say it has not been a success. Just to highlight the quality of football we have been privileged to watch, I have named my all-time Premiership XI. It has not been an easy task because we really have been spoiled for choice. But in 4-4-2 formation, these are the players who, in my view, have brought the most quality and enjoyment to our football. It was a tough task to pick out just 11 players from the Premiership years. I had to leave out such memorable performers as Eric Cantona, the unique Frenchman who played with such stylish arrogance; Gianfranco Zola, the little Italian who was a real bundle of tricks; Michael Owen, who still has plenty to offer if he is given an injury-free run, and Frank Lampard, the creative force of the Chelsea midfield.

Peter Schmeichel: The Great Dane was a goalkeeper who wanted to intimidate you, physically and mentally, from his position between the posts for Manchester United. He was big and brave and very loud. I had some great battles with him over the years. To see him closing down on you when you were through on goal was an awesome sight. You had to keep your nerve and not let him scare you into rushing your attempt to score. He was just as feared by his own defenders. He would let rip with a verbal volley at his colleagues if he did not feel they were doing their jobs properly and usually got the right reponse.

Gary Neville: He is the Mr Consistency of the Manchester United team. If you were to award him a mark out of ten for every match he would rarely slip below a seven. He lives for the Old Trafford cause. Gary is quick in the tackle and loves to get forward to supplement the attack. I was on the receiving end of many fine crosses from him when we were England colleagues and was very grateful for that. He is never short of an opinion, is Gary, and that has earned him a reputation for being the shop steward of the dressing room. There is nothing wrong with that. If you have something to say, then you should say it. I was never slow in coming forward with a view on anything if it was for the good of the team.

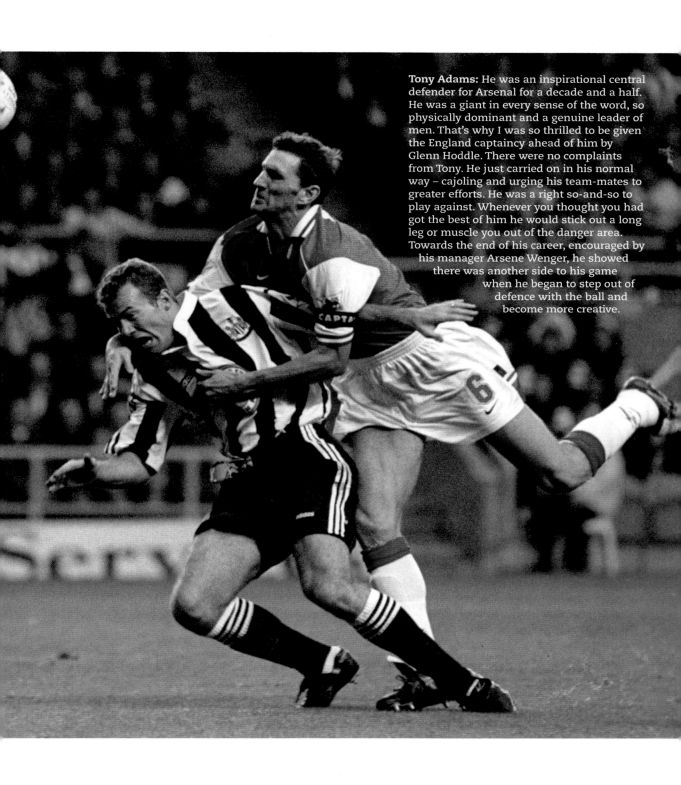

Tony Adams: He was an inspirational central defender for Arsenal for a decade and a half. He was a giant in every sense of the word, so physically dominant and a genuine leader of men. That's why I was so thrilled to be given the England captaincy ahead of him by Glenn Hoddle. There were no complaints from Tony. He just carried on in his normal way – cajoling and urging his team-mates to greater efforts. He was a right so-and-so to play against. Whenever you thought you had got the best of him he would stick out a long leg or muscle you out of the danger area. Towards the end of his career, encouraged by his manager Arsene Wenger, he showed there was another side to his game when he began to step out of defence with the ball and become more creative.

John Terry: He is out of the same mould as Tony Adams, tough, uncompromising and a great inspiration on and off the pitch. It says much for his qualities that he has been so prominent in a team full of world stars at Stamford Bridge. They have ploughed millions into making Chelsea one of the most high-profile clubs in the world and John has been their commander-in-chief and flag-bearer on the field. He is more skilful on the ball than most big centre-halves and an absolute nightmare to mark when he strides forward as an attacker into the opposition area for set pieces. He is one of the best headers of the ball I have ever come up against.

Stuart Pearce: They call him 'Psycho' but that doesn't do full justice to one of the most patriotic players every to set foot on an English football field. The mere sight of Stuart, bulging with muscles, wild-eyed and waving his fist, was enough to send you running for cover. You would certainly want him on your side in trench warfare. I will never forget his celebration when he converted his spot-kick in the shoot-out against Spain at Euro '96. He frightened the life out of me so I hate to think of the effect he had on opponents. But he wasn't just a bulldog who snapped and snarled his way through his career. He has a fine football brain and has made his impact already in club management.

David Beckham: He's the most talked about, photographed and controversial player of his generation and most of the attention that follows him has nothing to do with his outstanding football ability. I prefer to think of David as the best crosser of the ball I have ever seen. He didn't need blinding pace or outstanding trickery to get past his opponent. He had the knack of being able to whip over a cross with plenty of bend and swerve, delivering the ball in that area defenders hate – the space between the 'keeper and his back line. He scored some memorable goals from free-kicks for Manchester United, Real Madrid and England. He was dedicated enough to spend hours working on his skills after training. What a shame it would be if he was remembered for his showbiz lifestyle rather than his talent on the field. He has always had so much more to offer than that.

Steven Gerrard: He is the complete midfielder, who can run, tackle, scheme, score goals and provide the driving qualities that have made him such an outstanding skipper for Liverpool. It says a lot for his versatility that Anfield manager Rafael Benitez has tended to use him on the right side of his midfield four. Stevie has gone about his job without complaint even though it is clearly not his preferred position and he still manages to influence games heavily. Anyone who saw him drag Liverpool almost single-handedly from near-certain defeat in the Champions League final against AC Milan witnessed a master of the midfield art in action. I admire his commitment to the club he grew up supporting and still loves to this day.

Paul Scholes: You have to play in the same team as Paul to realise just how good a player he is. There are not many things he cannot do with a football, and if you add to that his energy and attitude you don't need much more from a midfielder. He has scored some outstanding goals of all varieties – headers, long-distance shots, one-on-ones with the 'keeper and close-range efforts after ghosting his way into the six-yard box. I think his early retirement from the England team has played no small part in our recent failures. You cannot just write off his contribution and hope to replace it through players of far less ability. But England's loss has definitely been United's gain and he proved himself as good as ever after his return from a serious eye problem.

Ryan Giggs: The Welshman is an absolute phenomenon who has reinvented the winger's role over the course of his 16 years as a first-team player at Old Trafford. He arrived on the scene as a lightning-quick youngster who could burn teams up with his pace. But over the seasons he has developed far more to his game. His work-rate is unbelievable and he has developed an appreciation of the game and tactical awareness that has made him an irreplaceable part of the United squad. He has the ability to drop deep or move inside to provide and convert chances. These are qualities that not many wingers can emulate in the modern game.

Thierry Henry: There was no overriding sense of anticipation when the Frenchman joined Arsenal from Juventus, where he had spent much of his career playing as a right winger. But Arsene Wenger clearly knew something no-one else had spotted. His conversion to a central striker was a master-stroke and, after a sluggish start in the Premiership, soon he was leaving defenders trailing behind him to become one of the most prolific scorers in Europe. Thierry is not your normal centre-forward. He is just as likely to pop up in a wide position to terrorise teams with his pace as he is to burst through the middle. I love his coolness in front of goal as well. He rarely panics when he is through with the 'keeper to beat.

Dennis Bergkamp: Thierry Henry described him as the best strike partner he has ever had – or ever will have – and compliments don't come much higher than that. The Dutchman had style, presence and composure. He could cause havoc with his positional play, dropping off deep into the area between midfield and attack, and defenders never quite knew how to handle him. He created so many goals for Henry, either with his passing skills or by making space for the French predator. Dennis could conjure up spectacular goals himself as well. I would have loved to have played alongside him.

6 THE ART OF
SCORING GOALS

DON'T ASK ME HOW I LEARNED THE ART OF SCORING GOALS. I CAN'T TELL YOU HOW I ARRIVED IN THE SIX-YARD BOX JUST AT THE RIGHT TIME TO CONVERT A CHANCE OR WHY I WOULD THROW MYSELF AMONG THE FLYING BOOTS AND BODIES TO GET A SNIFF OF GOAL. ALL I DO KNOW IS THAT I LOVED DOING IT AND DURING MY CAREER I NEVER GREW TIRED OF IT.

It didn't matter whether I was tapping one in from a few yards out, or blasting one home from 25 yards; the thrill was still the same. I loved the sensation of seeing the goalkeeper beaten by my shots or headers. I loved that wonderful ripple as the ball tore into the back of the net.

The joy of scoring goals came into my life at a very early age. I was kicking a ball about in the back garden with my dad as soon as I could walk and very quickly discovered I could strike the ball quite hard. It was not about physical power so I guess I had the natural gift of being able to strike my shots harder than most kids of my age.

When I started playing organised football that was a valuable asset. If you could kick it further and harder than the rest, it didn't half give you a head start. If you could strike it with power past the goalkeeper, the goals would soon start flowing in.

Over the years, of course, there was a lot more to discover about the art of being a striker and that came when I started going for proper training at Wallsend Boys Club and eventually joining Southampton as a trainee professional. But I do believe that instinct and natural ability for hitting the back of the net was something I was born with.

It brings its rewards and no member of the team attracts more attention or receives more adulation than the striker who grabs the match-winning goals. It's not an easy job. You have to be brave and physically strong and withstand the punishment of defenders whose job it is to stop you by fair means or foul. To have a big, ugly centre-half breathing down your neck and kicking lumps out of you is not a pleasant way to spend 90 minutes. But I never regretted a single moment of it and will always be proud of the goal-scoring records I achieved.

When I first burst on to the scene the excitement and adrenaline of playing first-team football carried me through. I was raw and fearless and was willing to run through brick walls to get myself a goal. I was not the quickest player around, though I was no slouch either. But I always reckoned that over the space of five yards, with the ball running loose in the penalty area, I was as fast as any Olympic 100-metres champion.

In time I had to modify my game because I was not as mobile as before. Age and the constant fight against injuries began to take their toll and I learned to become more astute and cunning with my positional play. I discovered how to manoeuvre centre-halves into areas they didn't want to be, and I suppose I became more of a team player. But I never lost that love for scoring, and right to my final match I never felt completely satisfied unless I came off the field with at least one goal under my belt.

The problem with drawing up any list of all-time favourites is that, almost immediately, you think of the ones you have omitted. For example how can any list be complete without mentioning Diego Maradona, the mercurial Argentinian, who many people regard as the greatest ever to have played the game. I never saw enough of him, certainly not in the flesh, to make a proper judgment of him but the clips I have seen illustrate what a unique talent he is.

He scored some truly amazing goals, notably the individual effort against England in the 1986 World Cup finals, and I can see why he is worshipped with almost a religious fervour by his thousands of fans. But with Maradona you have to have to accept the baggage that comes with him. For example on the day he scored that sensational solo goal against England he was also guilty of the infamous "Hand of God" goal when he clearly fisted the ball past Peter Shilton. On that occasion he cheated – and he admitted it. There have been other controversies surrounding him in the past, especially his notorious lifestyle, that have tended to tarnish his reputation.

Now I am not saying that footballers should be saints but I do think they have a responsibility to present themselves in an acceptable way for the millions of people who watch the game. For that reason alone the Argentinian doesn't make it onto my list.

Another absentee is the legendary Pele. Again I never saw too much of him because he was in his pomp when I was still a toddler. Talking to people

IT DIDN'T MATTER WHETHER I WAS TAPPING ONE IN FROM A FEW YARDS OUT, OR BLASTING ONE HOME FROM 25 YARDS; THE THRILL WAS STILL THE SAME.

about the Brazilian and watching old footage of him, I have come to recognise what a unique player he was. But I would have loved to have seen him in the flesh, studied him closely and made my own judgment of him rather than just rely on second hand information and fading film shots.

There have been many strikers over the years who have emerged as the greatest thing since sliced bread and who are going to take the world by storm. Michael Owen was one of those and despite his injuries he has stood the test of time and proved to be a truly world class performer. When Wayne Rooney burst onto the scene he received similar plaudits and the hype surrounding him was unfair.

But he lived up to it. It is amazing to think he was just 16-years–old when he made his debut for Everton and started scoring some sensational goals. He is simply phenomenal – strongly built, quick feet, pace and an astonishing football brain for one so young. In time Wayne could go on to become the best of the lot. But he has time on his side and if he continues to progress at the same rate, then he is going to be up there alongside Pele, Maradona and the all-time legends.

Wayne has got himself into the odd scrape off the field but I know he is a good lad. I spoke to him when he attended my testimonial dinner in Newcastle and he impressed me with his modest attitude and impeccable behaviour. The big thing he has in his favour is that he is working for Sir Alex Ferguson at Manchester United and I cannot think of any other manager better equipped to guide the career of the most gifted footballer of his generation.

As a fan of football and a so-called expert for the BBC, I enjoy my role now of analysing and discussing the development of players like Wayne Rooney. I know this for certain. It is a darn sight easier sitting in the comfort on a TV studio telling people how it should be done than being out there in the thick of the action as a striker when the boots and elbows are flying.

But you know what? Although I enjoy my life in retirement, I don't think I will ever find anything to replace the simple pleasure of putting the ball in the back of the net.

If I think long and hard I can just about remember every single one of the 422 goals I scored for my clubs and country. They are all special for different reasons and I shall store them away, treasure them and look back at them with pride as I grow older. It is a difficult task to pick out my all-time favourite, but these are my ten most memorable strikes.

1 **First of hat-trick on my full debut for Southampton v Arsenal . . . 9 April 1988:** I was still shaking like a leaf with nerves when Andy Townsend's cross came towards me. I got to it ahead of Michael Thomas and squeezed my header through goalkeeper John Lukic's legs. I hadn't worked out the one-arm-raised celebration at that stage of my career, so I just ran around flapping my arms about like an idiot. I could have jumped over the stands, I was so excited.

2 **First for England v France . . . 19 February 1992:** It was my full international debut and my first appearance on the hallowed Wembley turf. I was determined to savour every moment rather than let nerves take over. Just before half-time Nigel Clough took a corner, Mark Wright headed it down and I had to swivel inside the penalty area to sweep the ball into the net. I have relived that goal over and over and never tire of replaying it in my mind. I also set up a second for Gary Lineker in the second half.

**3 First for Blackburn v Crystal Palace . . .
15 August 1992:** There was a lot of pressure on
me on the day of my Blackburn entrance.
Rovers had paid a British record fee for me and
it seemed the whole country was watching to
see whether I was worth the money. I tried to
take the pressure off beforehand by saying
that no-one was worth that amount and my
price tag had nothing to do with me. There was
much relief when I smashed one past Nigel
Martyn from outside the box. I added a second
just for good measure.

**4 My 100th League goal for Blackburn v
Chelsea . . . 18 March 1995:** This was a
special milestone. Graeme Le Saux sent me
through and I had only goalkeeper Kevin
Hitchcock to beat, but he stood up and denied
me a good view of the target. So I decided to
smash it as hard as I could and the power of
the shot took him by surprise. Sometimes
brute force is as good a way as any and it paid
off for me this time.

5 My second in 4-1 win v Holland at Euro '96 . . . 18 June 1996: This was a team goal in every sense and summed up the best display I was ever involved in for England. Paul Gascoigne and Teddy Sheringham took part in an intricate passing movement and I finished it off with a shot that went in off the inside of the post. I remember thinking soon afterwards that a month earlier, when I was going through my so-called goal drought, it would have probably hit the woodwork and come back out.

6 Strike on home debut for
Newcastle v Wimbledon . . . 21
August 1996: This deserves a place
in my top ten because it was my first
wearing the black-and-white in front
of those amazing Geordie fans. It was
a good technical goal from a free-kick
just to the left of the Wimbledon
posts. I managed to get it up and
over the wall with just enough
bend on it to find the far corner
of the net. The place went mad.

7 **For England v Germany in 1-0 victory in Euro 2000 in Charleroi . . . 17 June 2000:** This was my last goal in open play for England and gave us our first victory over Germany in a competitive game for 34 years. David Beckham's free-kick reached me at the far post without any pace on it but I managed to loop it past Oliver Kahn. It won't go down as a particularly spectacular goal but it has immense sentimental value. I did score another from the penalty spot against Romania in the final group game but we lost 3-2 and went out of the tournament, after which I hung up my international boots.

8 **For Newcastle v Everton in 2-1 win at St James' Park . . . 1 December 2002:** They don't come much better than this where technique is concerned. There are times when you hit the ball so perfectly you know straight away that it is unstoppable. This was one of them. I was way outside the penalty area when the ball dropped to me and I volleyed it perfectly. It screamed into the top of the net and I have to say, in all modesty, that I am very proud of this goal.

9 **Breaking Jackie Milburn's record v Portsmouth in 2-0 win . . . 4 February 2006:** I have never experienced a feeling like the one I had when I scored this goal to beat Wor Jackie's record. It was not a spectacular one. I chased on to a backheeled pass from Shola Ameobi and raced away to beat Dean Kiely with a low shot. Jackie's record had stood for 50 years and now my name stands above his in the record books. I just hope I can live up to his reputation and his memory because, by all accounts, he was a very special person.

10 **Last goal of career v Sunderland, from penalty spot . . . 17 April 2006:** I have to get emotional over this one. I didn't know it was going to be my last goal because I didn't envisage myself getting injured and not playing another professional game. It was just a penalty but a special one. I didn't even think of missing it. I knew where I was going to put it and the Sunderland goalkeeper Kelvin Davis never stood a chance of saving it.

Goals come in all varieties and, likewise, strikers come in all shapes and sizes with different qualities. If you had to choose the ideal one he would have blinding pace, supreme aerial power, skills on the ball, vision, tactical know-how, and the ability to put the ball in the net from any distance. I doubt whether such a perfect specimen exists but over the years, as a fan and a player, I have studied the very best strikers, who have shown what it takes to do the hardest job in football. It's not just about putting the ball in the back of the net but it helps if you are a match-winner who knows his way to goal. My top ten favourite strikers all have that unique gift.

1 **Thierry Henry:** I have described elsewhere how the Arsenal striker has stamped his mark on the Premiership, not just with his goals output but with his own particular style. The Arsene Wenger way is to play a very controlled passing game and there is no-one better than his fellow Frenchman to add a cutting edge to it. His speed of movement and thought puts him at the sharp end of most of Arsenal's attacks and he can finish with the best of them. If he were able to score a few more scruffy tap-ins he would be capable of breaking every record in the book.

2 **Michael Owen:** From the moment he burst into the Liverpool and England teams as a fresh-faced teenager he has been one of the game's outstanding personalities. He received incredible exposure after the 1998 World Cup, with some people hailing him as the new Pele, but he never allowed that to get to his head. If only he had been able to steer clear of injuries he would have made an even bigger impression, but he has time on his side to prove himself as one of the great scorers. Nothing fazes Michael and no-one should be fooled by his sweet and innocent looks. He is a tough little so-and-so and determined to succeed.

3 **Dennis Bergkamp:** In my all-time Premiership X1, I described how this Dutch master was capable of many things. He has a magnificent football brain that allows him to spot openings that are not immediately obvious and his Arsenal mate Henry was able to cash in on that. But Bergkamp was also as strong as an ox and he could look after himself when the going got tough. No-one could intimidate him with the rough stuff and he could weigh in with his fair share of goals as well.

4 **Marco Van Basten:** I have seen the famous Holland international only on film, but what a player! He was probably the best volleyer of the ball there has ever been and to score goals at the rate he did in the ultra-defensive Italian League was an achievement in itself. There is endless footage of him smashing the ball into the net for AC Milan and Holland from all angles, including a hat-trick against England at Euro '88, and he is a perfect model for all strikers to follow. It is a pity that injury cut short his career.

5 **Eric Cantona:** I have this lasting image of
the Frenchman, with shirt-collar raised,
arrogantly looking around at the mere
mortals before him after he had scored
another spectacular goal for Manchester
United. He was massive in size and ability
and played the game with a strutting pride.
Cantona was another striker who did not
conform to the typical mould. He would drop
deep to play havoc with a team's marking
system, set up goals for others, score with
outrageous chips and flicks and get his fair
share from inside the six-yard box. He
finished playing too early but left some
marvellous memories behind.

6 **Ian Rush:** If you had to select the best finisher, the Welshman would have to be up there at the top of the pile. He made goal-scoring look so easy, which I assure you it isn't. How many times we have seen him bursting through for Liverpool and slotting the ball home as though he were going for a stroll in the park. But there were plenty of other aspects to his game. He had an astonishing work-rate and could time his runs into scoring positions like clockwork. He didn't quite hack it when he went to Italy to play for Juventus, but that was Liverpool's gain when he returned to Anfield.

7 **Kenny Dalglish:** After Rush it only seems natural to add the name Dalglish. They struck up such an incredible partnership and they complemented each other perfectly. One of my uncles took me to Anfield when I was young and I was mesmerised by the man they called King Kenny. But I only really began to appreciate how good he was when I joined Blackburn and he was my manager. He was usually the best player in training, long after his retirement. He had such a great first touch, was superb with his back to the goal and was blessed with vision that made you think he had eyes in the back of his head. He is a legend and they still sing his name at Anfield now.

8 **Mark Hughes:** They call him 'Sparky' and the sparks would usually fly when he was battling away up front for Manchester United and Wales. He had a tremendous physique for a striker, very strong in the upper body and enormous thighs. No-one could intimidate him. He took plenty of stick and handed plenty back. But don't let anyone run away with the idea that he was just a bulldozer. He could lead the front line superbly, holding the ball up while waiting for support, then laying it off to colleagues. He was good in the air and could volley goals in the style of Van Basten. He was a quiet bloke off the pitch and it has surprised some that he has moved so successfully into management.

9 **Gary Lineker:** I grew to rate the England striker during the World Cup tournament in Italy in 1990, when his goals took us to within touching distance of the final. He was quick and clinical around the box and thrived on little half-chances from rebounds. Gary was the ultimate professional who was always immaculately behaved and said the right things at the right time, but that hid the ruthlessly ambitious streak of a striker who would stop at nothing to get the ball in the back of the net. We are good mates and television colleagues now and he is just as professional in front of the cameras.

10   **Kevin Keegan:** He was my first idol. I
would arrive at St James' Park hours
before the kick-off to get a good place at
the Gallowgate End to watch him play. He
would never let me down. He gave 100 per
cent every game and produced the
magical moments that would send
thousands of kids like me home happy. If
there is one word to sum up Kevin it
would be attitude. His was always spot on.
He had great skill, tremendous charm,
enthusiasm and charisma but the one
thing that stood out was that he gave it his
all. Some say he was a manufactured
footballer. I don't go along with that, but if
he did strive to make himself a more
complete player then that makes him even
more special in my book.

7 THE GEORDIE NATION

I WAS WEARING A PAIR OF DARK GLASSES AND MY BASEBALL CAP WAS PULLED DOWN TO COVER MY FACE AS MY REPRESENTATIVE TONY STEPHENS DROVE ME ROUND THE SOUTHERN SUBURBS OF MANCHESTER.

Tony nipped in and out of several estate agents to pick up property details because I had more or less decided at that stage I would leave Blackburn Rovers and sign for Manchester United. My talks with Alex Ferguson had gone really well and the thought of playing for the world famous Old Trafford club was starting to grow on me.

I felt I had to leave Blackburn because I had gone as far as I could with them. We had won the title but I needed a fresh challenge to kick my career forwards. Jack Walker had promised me some time before that if I was ever unhappy at Rovers I could leave. I did not need to ask for anything in writing in the way of an escape clause. He gave me his word and that was good enough for me.

So once Tony had established that Manchester United, Newcastle United and Liverpool wanted me, I decided to seize the chance of seeing what each of the clubs had to offer. My meeting with Mr Ferguson (he hadn't been knighted by then) went superbly and the preliminary house hunting was a good indication as to what my future plans would be. But I still had to go and see the Newcastle manager Kevin Keegan to hear what he had to say. Again I wore dark glasses and my baseball cap when I met up with Kevin at a friend's house in Huddersfield. It all seems a bit cloak and dagger now but we had a secrecy agreement with Rovers that no-one would know of our discussions with other clubs and we didn't want to risk any leaks to the Press.

My meeting with Kevin was just as encouraging and I left him totally undecided about where or even whether I should move. I didn't meet the Liverpool manager Roy Evans but Tony had briefed me on what they had to offer and there was also some late interest from Everton. I had already ruled out moves to Juventus, Inter Milan and Barcelona because I didn't fancy uprooting my family to live abroad.

If I had been rushed into making a decision at that stage it would have been Manchester United or Liverpool with Newcastle a distant third choice. But before I made my mind up I wanted to tell Jack Walker face-to-face that I was leaving him. He sent over his private jet to fly me to his home in Jersey and all the way there I was having to prepare myself for the dreaded moment when I announced to him that I was leaving Rovers. He was not having it. He did everything in his power to persuade me to stay – including an offer to become Rovers player-manager and a contract that would heavily outweigh anything on the table from the other clubs. Gradually I began to change my mind about leaving Blackburn, especially when he asked me to give him one more year and then he would let me go with his blessing for a lower transfer fee. We even got to the stage where the terms were scribbled out on a piece of A4 paper but before anything was signed and formally agreed we had to leave before the airport at Jersey closed down for the night.

My mind was in a complete spin now. I had not got a clue about what I was going to do but by the time we had touched down at Blackpool Airport I had completed a u-turn and decided again that I had to leave Rovers for the sake of my career. The problem was where to?

My head was telling me Manchester United or Liverpool. My heart was saying Newcastle. I had hardly arrived back at my home in Formby when the phone went. It was Kevin Keegan telling me that he was going to the Far East the next day with the Newcastle squad and he wanted to have one more chat with me. For an hour he did the most magnificent selling job. When it comes to passion and persuasion Kevin has few equals. He sold me the idea of wearing the famous black and white No 9 shirt, the prospect of being idolised by those magnificent fans and the thought of filling my boyhood dreams while I still had the best years as a footballer ahead of me. I was already aware of everything Kevin was telling me but suddenly they all dropped into place and my mind was made up.

"I am going home," I told Lainya when I came off the phone from Kevin. Or at least I was hopping on the plane next day to the Far East to join up with the squad, leaving Lainya with the task of packing up all our belongings and preparing our move to the north east.

If I had any misgivings about my decision – and I didn't – they would have been dispelled when we returned from the Far East to my public unveiling at St. James' Park. The Geordie nation was out in force and in full voice. There were 15,000 fans waiting in the rain to see me officially sign the transfer

I HAD ALREADY RULED OUT MOVES TO JUVENTUS, INTER MILAN AND BARCELONA BECAUSE I DIDN'T FANCY UPROOTING MY FAMILY TO LIVE ABROAD.

forms taking me from Blackburn to Newcastle for £15.6million. I was back home after my football travels had taken me as a starry eyed kid to Southampton and on to a title winning adventure at Blackburn. But I wanted everyone in the north-east to know I was one of them. "The money and attention have not changed me, " I said above the roars on the crowd. "I am still just a sheet metal worker's son from Gosforth."

Home is where my heart lies and for 10 wonderful years I lived the dream to its full. People are still quick to remind me that I did not win a single piece of silverware in my time at Newcastle and that is my one regret – not for myself but for the amazing fans. If I have any disappointments it is that we under performed so badly in the two FA Cup finals we reached. In the 1998 final we were well beaten by Arsenal and the same thing happened a year later when we lost to Manchester United who were on the way to completing the treble. Not once, though, did I think it could have been me in a United shirt picking up Premiership, FA Cup and Champions League medals.

I will tell you what I got at Newcastle and it was priceless... the chance to wear the black and white No 9 shirt, the adulation of the most fanatical supporters in the world and the opportunity to break a scoring record that had stood unblemished for 50 years. Money could not buy the pleasure and pride that brought into my life.

Playing for Kevin Keegan was a rollercoaster ride. It was fun to be around the club when he was manager. Training was a delight and the quality of our football was outstanding at times. We pushed Manchester United all the way in my first season and hammered them 5-0 in a memorable game at St James' Park. We finished runners-up for the second time in a row. The goals kept flowing and the crowds just loved it.

Then completely out of the blue Kevin resigned. I still don't know to this day why he did it. Our first team coach Terry McDermott called us together before training one morning and announced out of the blue that the gaffer had quit. I know that Kevin is a man of great principle and if he felt something was not right at the club or believed he could not take it any further he would not hang around. He disappeared out of the lives of the

"THE MONEY AND ATTENTION HAVE NOT CHANGED ME," I SAID ABOVE THE ROARS OF THE CROWD. "I AM STILL JUST A SHEET METAL WORKER'S SON FROM GOSFORTH."

football fans but we have stayed close friends over the years. I love his company on the golf course and at race meetings and I still like to hear his views on football. His enthusiasm for life is as great as ever.

I was delighted when Kenny Dalglish took over because he was winner at Liverpool and Blackburn and I felt for sure he could do the same for Newcastle. It didn't work out simply because the players were not good enough. I suffered a serious injury at the start of the 1997 season that kept me out for half of the campaign and by the time I had returned, Kenny was under pressure as manager.

He was being criticised for making too many changes too quickly but I could not agree with that. Kevin had stated on his departure that he had taken the club as far as he could. So it was obvious that Kenny had to reshape the team, though he was not popular for selling crowd favourites like Les Ferdinand and Tino Asprilla. Besides no-one knew what kind of pressure he was under from within the club to stabilise the finances. Kenny will not be remembered with too much fondness on Tyneside but he was a top manager and still is a top bloke in my eyes. Kenny's strength was that he was a players' manager. He never criticised them in public and gave them complete loyalty. He expected the same in return.

The same could not be said of his replacement Ruud Gullit. Now I utterly respect what he did as a world class player and acknowledge that he had a wonderful career but things became impossible for us after he took over from Kenny as manager. I did not have a problem with him at first but gradually it became clear he wanted to confront me. He never said it to my face but having heard him claim after his departure that he thought I was the most over-rated player in the game, that tells you how he much he rated me – or rather didn't.

And it was not just me. Stuart Pearce, John Barnes and Rob Lee were all bombed out by him or shoved to one side. That suggests to me he might have had a problem with big name players who might challenge his ego. My turn to get the cold shoulder – along with Duncan Ferguson – came at an away game at Sunderland. I was left on the bench alongside big Dunc. He didn't even have the courtesy to tell me why I was left out. I read it on the notice board when the team sheet went up. The game ended in a 2-1 and Gullit pointed out sarcastically that the goals had been conceded after Dunc and I were sent on as subs. Next morning I decided to have it out with the manager.

Dunc had beaten me to it and the door to the manager's office was already off its hinges when I got to the training ground. Let's just say we had a frank exchange of views. It pains me to admit this but if Gullit had stayed at Newcastle I would have left. It would have broken my heart but I could not have stayed and given my all for that manager. It would have been unfair to the club. In any case friends have since told me that he had been talking to John Gregory about selling me to Aston Villa.

Fortunately, Gullit resigned and Bobby Robson came in to replace him. It was chalk and cheese. Bobby is a Geordie who knows the club, loves the fans and appreciates what it takes to make them happy. His first home game was against Sheffield Wednesday and we won 8-0. I scored five and I think that tells you all you need to know about the change of mood in the dressing room. Bobby took us from the relegation zone to third in the table within the space of two years. That was some achievement but just as important as the results was that he put a smile back on the faces of the fans.

The Geordies are not mugs. They know what is acceptable from their team and they love to see the game played with a bit of style and swagger. Bobby gave them that along with Champions League football but unfortunately not the trophy they craved so much. When he was replaced by Graeme Souness, there was still a great deal of affection for the former England manager among the supporters.

Graeme was another manager who wore his heart on his sleeve and didn't mince his words. That led to him falling out with one or two players publicly – notably Craig Bellamy. After a good start the fans turned on him and the mood of the club was downbeat again when he left in the early part of 2006.

I had announced that I was going to retire at the end of that season. I was feeling the strain of having to play a couple of matches every week and I had always insisted I didn't want to end up as a tired old has-been who remained in the game for too long. But as the season progressed I started to enjoy my football even more and people around me were urging me to give it another year. In the end I agreed, though I only thought I would have a bit part to play in the 2005-06 season.

But with Michael Owen injured I found myself thrust more and more into playing a major role and gradually Jackie Milburn's club scoring record began to loom closer. Some people thought I only stayed on to break Wor Jackie's record but that was not the case. I never intended to play in as many games as I did and believe me there were times when my body was screaming out to me to have a break.

But as the record approached I got caught up in the euphoria of it all. When goal number 201 went in against Portsmouth on 4 February 2006, it felt as good as anything I have ever achieved in football. The ovation from the fans seemed to never stop. It is something that will live with me forever.

I am not an emotional person but there was a big lump in my throat that day and I lived on the adrenalin of it for weeks.

I would like to say my Newcastle career ended in a moment of glory with me being carried shoulder high from the field by my team-mates. Unfortunately it didn't quite work out like that. I left the stage flat out on a stretcher with a knee injury that later turned out to be a torn medial knee ligament. I had still managed to score my 206th goal from the penalty spot that day against Sunderland as a little parting shot. There were three games left of the season and I spent them on the sidelines as coaching assistant alongside Glenn Roeder who had been appointed to replace Graeme Souness.

It seemed strange standing there knowing that I would not play another game for Newcastle – or anyone else for that matter. Football had consumed and enriched my life and there was a slight feeling of emptiness but it did not last for long. I still had my goodbyes to say and a life to plan outside the game.

When people ask me why it is that Newcastle have not achieved any real success as a football club I tend to be stuck for an answer. It is a bit like England as an international force in a way. We have had so many good players representing the country but still have not been able to pull off a major tournament since the World Cup in 1966. It's a real mystery.

I think what is needed is some stability in the manager's office. There has been too much chopping and changing over the years and that has not lent itself to the level of consistency that tends to bring success. Look at the top clubs and you see long serving managers who have been given time to develop their strategies and build winning teams. You have to be patient through the bad times. The best example of this was at Manchester United who stuck firmly behind Sir Alex Ferguson during the early days. It would have been easy to sack him back then but they remained loyal and were rewarded with one of the most successful periods in their famous history.

Newcastle need to show the same faith in their manager – once they have established who is the right man for the job. The problem is discovering the right person to satisfy the overwhelming desire of the supporters to see their club on top of the pile. It will take a big man to do it and when Newcastle find him they have to stick with him.

Will it be Alan Shearer one day? Well not in the foreseeable future. It is no secret that I could have been given the job not long after my retirement but the time was not right for me. I still had other things I wanted to do in my life away from the game. But in the future? I do fancy a crack at management at some stage but only when I feel ready and qualified to accept the challenge, I prefer not to dwell on it until the occasion arises.

Newcastle wanted to wait for the club's return from a tour to the Far East before holding the official press conference to announce my transfer. It was a superb gesture because it gave the Geordie fans the chance to share the moment. The club's president Sir John Hall and the boss Kevin Keegan shared the top table with me as I answered the media's questions.

Once the formalities were complete I stepped outside to be greeted by an amazing sight. It was mid-afternoon on a Monday in the pouring rain, but thousands turned out to welcome me back home. Many of them must have taken the day off work and if I needed any proof of their fanatical support I got it that day.

You expect them to turn up in great numbers to watch a game but this was just to confirm my transfer from Blackburn. Already I had no doubts that I had made the right decision to refuse the chance to join either Manchester United or Liverpool, and this underlined the rightness of what I had done. I was delighted to be with my own folk.

If I had been told then that I would spend the next ten years at Newcastle I would have thought the notion was a bit far-fetched but, with the very occasional exception, I enjoyed every minute of it.

I opened my scoring account for Newcastle at Wimbledon from a free-kick just outside the penalty area. This was a favourite spot for me because I always fancied blasting the ball past the'keeper from around 20 yards.

But this goal contained a bit more finesse and that is something you could not say about me too often. It is quite an art to get the ball up over the defensive wall and then get it to dip underneath the crossbar. It needed a bit of swerve and power on the shot to get it beyond the 'keeper.

It all came right for me that day and you can tell
from my reaction how thrilled I was to get off the
mark. I expected to score goals for Newcastle but
it was nice to get that first one under my belt.

To beat Manchester United is always a big achievement but when we hammered them 5-0 in the 1996-97 season it was a day never to forget. Kevin Keegan went for broke with an attacking force that included Les Ferdinand, David Ginola, Peter Beardsley and myself. It would have been difficult for anyone to live with us that day.

Kevin loved to see all-out attack, often to his downfall, but when it came off it was spectacular to watch. To make it even sweeter United had beaten us 4-0 at the start of the season in the Charity Shield, so this was pay-back time.

Kevin Keegan's retirement sent shock waves through the city and no-one really knows to this day why he walked away from a job when it seemed he had so much more to achieve.

Kevin has become a good mate of mine but I did not feel it was right for me to ask why he went. If he had wanted to tell me he would have done so. There had been no inkling of it beforehand. He was going about his job quite normally.

But Kevin was the sort of guy who would not hang around for the sake of it if he felt everything was not the way he wanted it. Likewise, if he believed he had taken the team as far as was possible, he would decide it was time to move on.

It was as much of a surprise to the players as it was to the supporters when he went. Terry McDermott called us together at the training ground one Monday morning to break the news to us. There was a stunned silence but then we had to get on with our jobs. No matter how popular Kevin was among the players, the show had to go on without him.

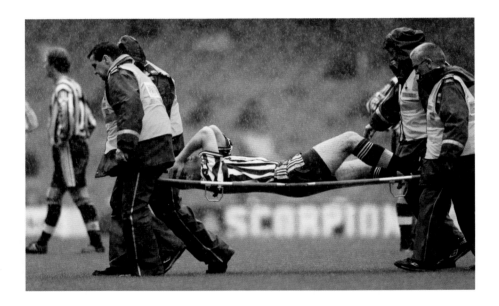

It looks as if I had just been hit by a Graeme Souness tackle. It meant another injury lay-off and I hated every minute I was out of action. I love to watch football but never enjoyed those games that I should have been involved in. I kicked every ball and was itching to get out there.

If there is anything worse in football than losing an FA Cup final at Wembley, I never discovered it. Often it's said that it's great to be part of a cup final occasion whatever the result, but I don't go along with that. Wembley is no place for losers.

We did not do ourselves justice in the 1998 final against Arsenal but I did hit the post and Nikos Dabizas cracked the crossbar. A goal at either of those moments could have put us back in the game, but it was not to be.

Arsenal were flat out to complete the League and FA Cup double that day and were an irresistible force. I just felt bitterly disappointed for the fans who believed our long wait for a major cup triumph was about to end.

Above: David Seaman offers his commiserations at the final whistle. **Right:** David Batty has run himself into the ground and I am wandering around like a lost soul.

The least said about my relationship with Ruud
Gullit the better. You would have to ask him
why we didn't get on because I don't have a clue.
I thought he was a very good coach who had
plenty to offer. He was a big personality with
good ideas but he rubbed quite a few players
up the wrong way.

I felt it was clear at one stage that he didn't want
me at the club and, as much as it would have
broken my heart, I had resigned myself to leaving.
Fortunately he went first and my love affair with
Newcastle continued.

Another FA Cup final and another defeat. This time it was 1999 and Manchester United were in hot pursuit of the treble of Premiership title, FA Cup and Champions League.

They went on to complete their hat-trick while we were left licking our wounds again. We didn't produce what we were capable of but, after losing to double-chasing Arsenal a year earlier, it was just our luck to come up against a United side who were just as unstoppable.

The FA Cup final is a great day out for everyone? Don't you believe it! Not if you are on the wrong end of a beating. Manchester United battered us and, as you can see from these pictures, I found the defeat hard to live with.

For the second year running our supporters were magnificent. When we got back home to Newcastle they lined the streets of the city and gave us a heroes' welcome. Imagine what it would be like if we actually won something.

We are still waiting for that to happen and when it does I want to be there because it will be well worth witnessing.

This was the only sending-off of my career and it came in almost laughable circumstances against Aston Villa at the start of the 1999-2000 season. Actually I was dismissed a couple of years earlier against Charlton but that was later rescinded by the FA.

Referee Uriah Rennie seemed to take great delight in carding me for an alleged elbowing offence against Villa. Even some of the Villa players had a snigger among themselves over that decision.

I have always maintained it is impossible to jump up for a header without raising your arms for leverage and to give yourself some extra protection. If your arms accidentally brush an opponent, that doesn't make it a deliberate assault.

In those situations you have to rely on your opponent to behave with some honesty and stay on his feet, and the referee to spot what has gone on. I think I was hard done by on both counts against Villa.

Sir Bobby Robson is a phenomenal football personality. We all saw that for ourselves when he took over from Ruud Gullit as Newcastle manager. There could have been no better appointment at that particular time.

It is fair to say that he transformed the whole mood of the club when he joined us in 1999. We were despondent and in real danger of dropping out of the Premiership before he arrived. Personally, I have never felt so low in my career.

But Bobby breezed in and, at the age of 66, breathed some new life into the place. He was as enthusiastic as a teenager and loved turning up at the training ground each day to put the players through their paces.

He gave me back my enthusiasm for the game and put a smile on everyone's faces. He was much travelled as a coach and a manager, and his experience and zest for life helped to take us from near the bottom of the table into Europe within the space of a few years. He will always have a special place in the hearts of all Geordies.

Newcastle's 8-0 victory over Sheffield Wednesday in 1999 was the most perfect way to illustrate the effect Sir Bobby Robson had on us when he took over as manager. It felt as if a great weight had been lifted off me and I went on a personal scoring spree.

It was Bobby's first home game in charge and the relief was there for all to see as I plundered five goals – the most I ever scored in one game. That wasn't bad for a player who was not considered good enough to make the starting line-up by Ruud Gullit.

I put the ball in the net for our third goal in the space of 11 minutes. The response from players and fans alike showed there was a new mood of optimism around the place.

The 300th League goal of my career came against
Arsenal from a free-kick just outside the box.
There was nothing very subtle about this one. It
was just brute force that took the ball into the net
as I gave it the full treatment.

I can remember just about every goal I have
scored but the milestones like this one are usually
brought to my attention by the media.

The Freedom of the City of Newcastle was granted to me by the City Council in 2001 and for the sheet-metal worker's son from Gosforth it was an immensely proud moment. Apparently it gives me the right to graze my cattle on Town Moor, common land just outside the city centre. I haven't taken advantage of that particular privilege yet!

I love everything about Newcastle but what sets it apart from everywhere else is its people. They love their football and they love to work and play hard. I have found it difficult to step out into the city at times during the day because it creates too much of a stir, but I can go out at night to a restaurant without being hassled by the supporters.

I realise that I have a responsibility to these people who have helped pay my wages and given me a great life from football, so what's wrong with signing a few autographs? My view is that the time to start worrying is when they stop asking you.

It can be a tough and lonely life as a striker when you play up front against defenders whose only aim is to leave their mark on you. The treatment I received in this game against Manchester City was typical of the punishment you have to endure. The secret is not to retaliate. The best way to get your own back against opponents who try to kick lumps out of you is not to get involved in a war, but to score goals against them. That makes all the bumps and bruises worthwhile.

Manchester United captain Roy Keane and I enjoyed this close encounter at St James' Park. All I did was stand in front of him to stop him taking a quick throw-in and he didn't take too kindly to it – probably because we were winning 4-3 with a few minutes to play. He threw a right-hander at me but I saw it coming and swayed out of the way. The lack of contact did not stop Roy getting a red card, nor did it diminish my admiration for him as a player. He had great energy, a terrific engine and a winning mentality – my idea of a perfect midfielder, even though his temperament got the better of him at times. His first move into management, at Sunderland, offered further proof of what a talented football competitor he is.

Graeme Souness was unfortunate in that he had to follow a highly popular figure in Bobby Robson into the manager's hot seat at St James' Park. The fans never really took to him and that was a shame.

It was a bit like that when Kenny Dalglish succeeded Kevin Keegan. It is so difficult to take over from someone who was idolised by the supporters. Both Kenny and Graeme were great players and managers in their own right. Maybe they were just around at the wrong time.

I saw Graeme as a player and his qualities on the field were the same as those off it. He was open, honest, very tough and extremely fair. But I never thought the fans took to him from the start and that was a great shame because he was desperate to bring us success.

This was another career milestone – my 200th Premiership goal, which came against Charlton in April 2002. Lomano Lua-Lua helps me to celebrate.

I finished with a total of 260 goals in the Premiership and, at the time of writing, Andy Cole was second on the all-time list with 185. Will my total ever be overtaken? Well, all records are there to be broken, and whoever does it will have had a long and satisfying career.

I always thought Thierry Henry and Michael Owen would come close, but unfortunately they have both been sidelined for long spells due to injuries, and that has damaged their chances.

In one of the most bizarre incidents of my career, I finished up with a busted nose after an accidental clash with one of my best mates, Rob Lee, who had left Newcastle to join Derby.

We had agreed to go out for a meal afterwards with our wives, who both watched in disbelief as we lay on the ground with blood pouring from our head wounds.

We still went for the meal, and the blessing in disguise for me was that, while resetting my nose, the surgeon was able to cure a nosebleed problem that had dogged me for several years.

It took me ten seconds to score this goal against Manchester City, the joint-fastest in Premiership history. City kicked off and played the ball back to goalkeeper Carlo Nash. I ran towards him to put him under pressure and he kindly cleared the ball to my feet. If only they had all been that easy.

When the Premiership celebrated its tenth anniversary there were awards for the outstanding players since the league was formed. I was named player of the decade, with Eric Cantona getting the overseas player prize. We both also made it into the team of the decade.

The Frenchman was unique on and off the field. His strutting style made him a showman to be admired. More importantly, he was so effective as a striker capable of scoring outstanding goals and creating them, too. Not many footballers would have survived to tell the tale after leaping over the barriers to assault a fan like he did at Crystal Palace. He was unpredictable and a great loss to the Premiership when he decided to call it a day.

I have never known such pain as when I was carried from the field during a game against Chelsea in a pre-season tournament at Goodison Park. With no-one near me, I caught my foot in the turf and, as well as damaging ankle ligaments, I cracked a bone in my leg and dislocated my ankle.

It left me on the sidelines for several months and, believe me, there is nothing so soul-destroying as that. The gymnasium can be the loneliest place on earth as you struggle to recover from a serious injury. It happened to me too many times.

All you can do is set yourself little targets week by week and gradually build up your fitness levels. The worst thing is to watch the other players enjoying themselves out on the training pitch. You feel an outsider and it is just as bad on match days. You have worked hard in the gym all week, yet when Saturday comes you have nothing to show for your efforts.

Michael Owen has become a very good pal of mine, and as well as being a great lad he is a top striker. As soon as I saw him excelling as a 17-year-old, I knew he was a real talent who would serve England for many years. At the World Cup in France as a raw teenager, he made everyone sit up and take notice of him with his wonder goal against Argentina.

I was fortunate enough to play alongside him for England and Newcastle and saw at first hand how he could terrorise defences with his pace and power. He makes goal-scoring look easy. I won't harp on about his injuries any more because I know how frustrating it is to be ruled out of action.

Goal number 200 for Newcastle enabled me to equal the great Jackie Milburn's record. It came against Mansfield Town in the FA Cup, and from whatever angle you look at it in the pictures above, it was another spine-tingling moment in my last season for Newcastle.

Above: The record finally came after I had
gone four games without a goal, but it was worth
the wait. I hit No 201 against Portsmouth on
4 February 2006 and St James' Park went mad.
So did I for a few moments.

Opposite top: The applause lasted for a good ten
minutes and it was difficult to concentrate on the
game for a while. One of the most memorable
features of breaking the record was the reaction
I got from the Milburn family.

I received a lovely message from Jackie's widow
Laura, who was kind enough to tell me that her
husband would have been thrilled that I had
beaten his total. It had stood for 49 years and just
to be mentioned in the same bracket as a true
legend and a real gentleman was too much to
take in.

Opposite bottom: These boots are made for
scoring... my suppliers Umbro made this
commemorative pair to mark my achievement of
breaking Jackie Milburn's record.

Sadly, this is where it all came to an end. Goal No 206 for Newcastle arrived against Sunderland in what proved to be my last game for the club. It was quite a pressurised situation because I had missed a penalty against them a couple of seasons earlier and I dreaded missing another. It was to be my second-last touch of the ball in the Premiership because I collapsed in a heap soon afterwards and did not kick another ball in anger.

I knew straight away that my time was up. I had suffered enough injuries to know when one was serious. The medial ligament in my left knee had snapped and it was curtains for my career.

It was only when I got back to the dressing room that the reality hit me, but I managed to look on the bright side. I reflected on the facts that we had beaten our local rivals 4-1 and that I had scored in my last game as a professional. It was time to move on.

8 RETIREMENT REFLECTION
AND THE FUTURE

IT WAS ABOUT THE TIME THAT PLAYERS WERE STARTING BACK FOR PRE-SEASON TRAINING, AROUND JULY 2006, THAT IT FINALLY SUNK IN. I WAS NOT A PROFESSIONAL FOOTBALLER ANY MORE. I WAS LYING BY A POOL BATHED IN SUNSHINE AND THINKING OF THE OTHER LADS POUNDING AWAY ON THE ROADS AND AROUND THE TRAINING GROUND.

Of course, there was a tinge of regret that the game I loved was no longer the focal point of my life. But I have to be honest and say I did not miss the grind of that pre-season work. I was never the greatest runner over long distances and my body was certainly thankful that it did not have to be punished during another gruelling six-week period before the season started.

Sure, I missed the banter in the dressing room and on match days. That was always one of the perks of the job for me. There is a unique comradeship and humour that is impossible to replace. But for the first time in 18 years I could look forward to doing exactly what I wanted to do. I have other commitments, like being an ambassador for my kit suppliers Umbro, and for Newcastle United, and my work as a pundit for the BBC.

But now I can spend real quality time with my family and I intend to make the most of it. For example, recently I was able to enjoy a skiing holiday with my wife and kids during one of the school breaks. That was something I could not have dreamed about when I was playing because of the obvious risk of injuries. It was great fun. Suddenly it felt like I was a new person able to enjoy my freedom, rather than being told what to do and when to do it. Regular games of golf and visits to the races could be arranged without having to consult the fixture list and training schedules.

If that sounds like I had any regrets about my life as a footballer then it shouldn't. From my first day at Southampton right through to my last Premiership appearance for Newcastle against Sunderland, I loved every minute of it. In fact, it lasted a bit longer than that. My testimonial match against Celtic on 11 May 2006 was my final appearance in front of the Geordie fans and it still makes the hairs stand up on the back of my neck when I think about it. There were 52,000 of them packed into St James' Park and if I could have gone around and shaken the hand of every one of them I would have done so. I was only able to hobble around that night because

I was still recovering from my knee injury, but I did manage to get on to the pitch right at the end to score from a penalty that won us the game. That was just a bit of fun – but it was still a thrill to depart from the scene with a goal under my belt.

I limped away into a new life knowing there was a huge gap to fill but looking forward to a different kind of fulfilment. The BBC had been kind enough to offer me a contract to work on the Match of the Day programme and the England international games. I enjoy my television work immensely. People tell me I have become more interesting as a pundit now that I have stopped playing. That may be so. I do feel able to speak more openly about the game now that I am not directly involved, but I would never be controversial just for the sake of it. I try to give an open and honest opinion without causing offence.

Interestingly, I was contacted by Steve McClaren soon after his appointment as England coach and he asked me if I wanted to be part of his backroom team. It was a fascinating offer, especially as Terry Venables was also going to be involved, but I declined. I had already agreed to the BBC role and didn't want to break my contract with them. I also felt I needed to step back a bit from the professional game for a while. I needed the break from football and did not think the time was right to take on a coaching role, even in a part-time capacity.

As for my future in coaching and management, it is a question of wait and see. At the time of writing, I am still doing my coaching badges and I think that should tell you it is something I will consider one day. I want to be sure I am completely ready to devote my full attention to the job if and when I do commit myself to football management. During the time I was injured at the end of my last season, I was able to sit alongside Glenn Roeder on the bench for a few games and offer him my support. It afforded me a different way of viewing the game and I am sure that will stand me in good stead eventually.

For now I am happy to enjoy a reasonably pressure-free lifestyle. Certainly I would not rule out a return to the game at some point, but I have enough memories from football to last me a lifetime and it's nice to be able

I AM AMONG MY OWN FOLK ON TYNESIDE. IF YOU DON'T COME FROM THE AREA YOU WOULD NEVER REALLY APPRECIATE WHAT IT MEANS TO BE A PART OF THIS COMMUNITY.

to reflect on those for the time being. I still recall how it all started, learning my trade under Dave Merrington and Chris Nicholl and building on the values of hard work, good manners and decency that were instilled into me by my mum and dad.

It has been a great journey for the sheet-metal worker's son from Gosforth, who was able to visit Buckingham Palace to receive an OBE and was granted the freedom of the City of Newcastle. And while it is nice travelling the world, meeting high-profile dignitaries from all walks of life, I am happiest when I am among my own folk on Tyneside. If you don't come from the area you would never really appreciate what it means to be a part of this community. To be their local hero is beyond description.

I feel as if I am one of them even more now that I am not playing. I was unable to help bring any trophies to the club and that is a real regret. We always fell that little bit short in the Premiership, FA Cup and Europe. But one thing is for certain. If there is any justice in football, Newcastle United will triumph one day. And I will be there leading the cheering in among the greatest fans in the world.

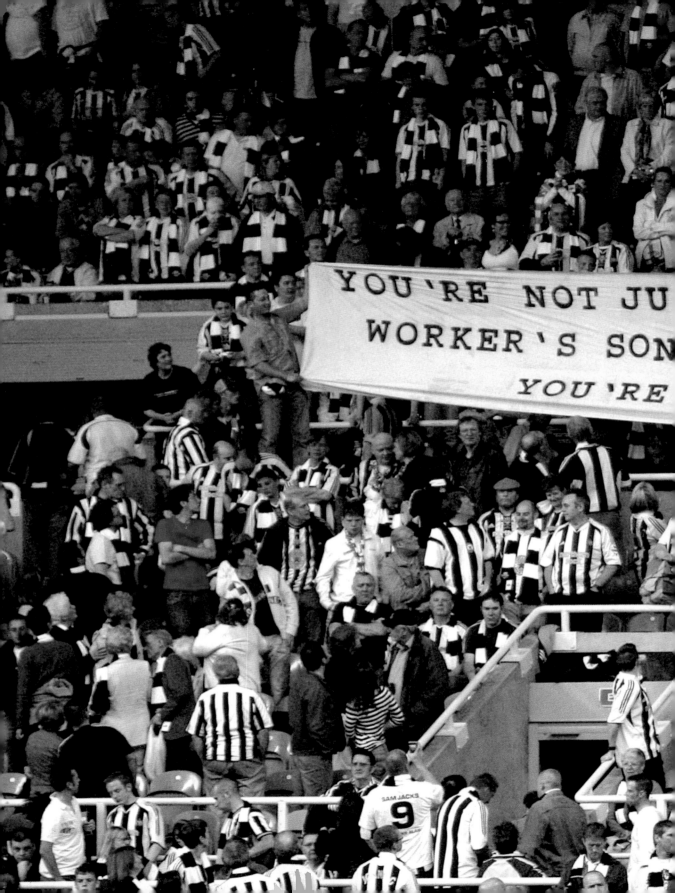

It was not often that my family stepped on to centre-stage but at my testimonial game at St James' Park, I felt it was only fair that they joined me to say my final farewell to the fans. My wife Lainya, daughters Chloe and Hollie and son Will soaked up the atmosphere. The noise was a bit to loud for young Will's ears but it made me realise how much I would miss the roar of the crowd.

St James' Park is a magnificent arena, though it has changed incredibly since I first started visiting it as a young boy. There is no better sight than to see it packed to the rafters on a match day.

The fans turned out in their thousands on 11 May 2006 to say their goodbyes to me at my testimonial game against Celtic, and we tried to make sure they got value for money. It was only a tiny gesture but on each seat we placed a black-and-white commemorative scarf for the supporters to take home as a keepsake.

I was able to hobble on to the pitch in the final few minutes of the match to knock in a penalty that, by pure coincidence, was awarded to Newcastle. It was only a bit of fun, but oddly enough I got that same old buzz from seeing the ball nestle in the back of the net.

Perhaps it would give me the urge to change my mind and give it one more season for old times' sake? Would it heck! I had completed my ten years and there could be no better way to bow out than to the acclaim of a full house, with a host of glorious memories and scoring records to take with me into my retirement.

SHEARER TESTIMONIAL 2006

'I'm a celebrity, get me out of here!' I could have been saying that to television presenters Ant and Dec, but in fact I was expressing my gratitude to everyone who showed up for my testimonial, and my eternal thanks to them for helping me to live the dream that just seemed to go on and on.

Prime Minister Tony Blair was kind enough to travel up to the north-east to help to hand over the proceeds of my testimonial to national and local charities. When all the fund-raising was complete, and all the sums added up, the total came to £1,640,000, and that was a staggering amount. It was also a glowing tribute to all the people who worked so hard putting together the various events.

It was not difficult to decide to give the money to charity. The hard part was deciding which charities should benefit. In the end I split it between national and local causes, including the Bobby Moore Fund for Cancer Research, the National Society for the Prevention of Cruelty to Children, three local hospitals and my first junior teams, Cramlington Juniors and Wallsend Boys Club.

Above: My OBE is one of my most treasured possessions, and I was privileged to receive it in the Queen's Birthday Honours List in 2001. To make the day complete, Lainya and daughters Hollie and Chloe joined me when I accepted the award from Her Majesty at Buckingham Palace.

Left: It was nice to get the royal seal of approval from Her Majesty the Queen when she invited me to Buckingham Palace after the World Cup finals in 1998. Jamaican captain Warren Barrett and Scotland skipper Colin Hendry completed the gathering, with Prince Philip also in attendance.

Retirement has meant I have been able to spend more quality time with my family. These are some of the snaps taken during my career, capturing rare and precious moments. I am delighted now to be able to be at home more, watching the children grow up and putting Lainya first rather than a poor second behind football.

Football folk rarely miss a chance to hone their golf skills. Here the Newcastle club doctor, Roddy McDonald, shows his putting style in the grounds of a hotel on an away trip in front of an appreciative audience.

Golf has always been a real passion for me. If I had not been a professional footballer I would have loved to have made a career out of my second-favourite sport. It's wonderful to switch off my mobile phone and get out into the open air with my clubs. Certainly it was always a great escape from the occasionally mad world of football.

Above left: Nick Faldo was a big favourite of mine. I loved his dedication, his determination and his obsession to keep on improving his game. It was a pleasure to enjoy a round with him at Gleneagles.

Above, top right: Colin Montgomerie was another personal favourite. He was a big football fan and here he joins me in the Newcastle dressing room.

Above, bottom right: I was lucky to share the fairways with some of the top pros, including the Swedish Ryder Cup star Jesper Parnevik in a pro-am tournament at Roxborough.

I am in good company here with my BBC
colleague and former England striker Gary
Lineker at an official dinner. I did not get much
chance to play alongside Gary, since his
international career was coming to an end
just as mine was getting started.

I was awarded an Honorary Doctorate of Civil Law at Northumbria University in 2006, though if anyone is looking for legal representation I don't suggest they engage me to defend them. It was quite an achievement for someone who left secondary school with a single GCSE pass in English oral. Some of my so-called friends reckon the headgear was perfect for covering up my receding hairline.

STATISTICS

SENIOR CLUB CAREER SEASON BY SEASON

1987/88
Southampton – 12th in Division 1
manager Chris Nicholl
League: 3 (2) games, 3 goals
Total: 3 (2) games, 3 goals

1988/89
Southampton – 13th in Division 1
manager Chris Nicholl
League: 8 (2) games, 0 goals
Total: 8 (2) games, 0 goals

1989/90
Southampton – 7th in Division 1
manager Chris Nicholl
League: 19 (7) games, 3 goals
FA Cup: 1 (2) games, 0 goals
League Cup: 4 (2) games, 2 goals
Total: 24 (11) games, 5 goals

1990/91
Southampton – 14th in Division 1
manager Chris Nicholl
League: 34 (2) games, 4 goals
FA Cup: 3 (1) games, 2 goals
League Cup: 6 games, 6 goals
Zenith Data Systems Cup: 2 games, 2 goals
Total: 45 (3) games, 14 goals

1991/92
Southampton – 16th in Division 1
manager Ian Branfoot
League: 41 games, 13 goals
FA Cup: 7 games, 2 goals
League Cup: 6 games, 3 goals
Zenith Data Systems Cup: 6 games, 3 goals
Total: 60 games, 21 goals

1992/93
Blackburn Rovers – 4th in Premiership
manager Kenny Dalglish
League: 21 games, 16 goals
League Cup: 5 games, 6 goals
Total: 26 games, 22 goals

1993/94
Blackburn Rovers – 2nd in Premiership
manager Kenny Dalglish
League: 34 (6) games, 31 goals
FA Cup: 4 games, 2 goals
League Cup: 4 games, 1 goal
Total: 42 (6) games, 34 goals

1994/95
Blackburn Rovers – 1st in Premiership
manager Kenny Dalglish
League: 42 games, 34 goals
FA Cup: 2 games, 0 goals
League Cup: 3 games, 2 goals
Europe: 2 games, 1 goal
Total: 49 games, 37 goals

1995/96
Blackburn Rovers – 7th in Premiership
manager Ray Harford
League: 35 games, 31 goals
FA Cup: 2 games, 0 goals
League Cup: 4 games, 5 goals
Europe: 6 games, 1 goal
Charity Shield: 1 game, 0 goals
Total: 48 games, 37 goals

1996/97
Newcastle United – 2nd in Premiership
manager Kevin Keegan, then Kenny Dalglish
League: 31 games, 25 goals
FA Cup: 3 games, 1 goal
League Cup: 1 game, 1 goal
Europe: 4 games, 1 goal
Charity Shield: 1 game, 0 goals
Total: 40 games, 28 goals

1997/98
Newcastle United – 13th in Premiership
manager Kenny Dalglish
League: 15 (2) games, 2 goals
FA Cup: 6 games, 5 goals
Total: 21 (2) games, 7 goals

1998/99
Newcastle United – 13th in Premiership
manager Kenny Dalglish, then Ruud Gullit
League: 29 (1) games, 14 goals
FA Cup: 6 games, 5 goals
League Cup: 2 games, 1 goal
Europe: 2 games, 1 goal
Total: 39 (1) games, 21 goals

1999/2000
Newcastle United – 11th in Premiership
manager Ruud Gullit, then Bobby Robson
League: 36 (1) games, 23 goals
FA Cup: 6 games, 5 goals
League Cup: 1 game, 0 goals
Europe: 6 games, 2 goals
Total: 49 (1) games, 30 goals

2000/01
Newcastle United – 11th in Premiership
manager Bobby Robson
League: 19 games, 5 goals
League Cup: 4 games, 2 goals
Total: 23 games, 7 goals

2001/02
Newcastle United – 4th in Premiership
manager Bobby Robson
League: 36 (1) games, 23 goals
FA Cup: 5 games, 2 goals
League Cup: 4 games, 2 goals
Total: 45 (1) games, 27 goals

2002/03
Newcastle United – 3rd in Premiership
manager Bobby Robson
League: 35 games, 17 goals
FA Cup: 1 game, 1 goal
Europe: 12 games, 7 goals
Total: 48 games, 25 goals

2003/04
Newcastle United – 5th in Premiership
manager Bobby Robson
League: 37 games, 22 goals
FA Cup: 2 games, 0 goals
League Cup: 0 (1) game, 0 goals
Europe: 12 games, 6 goals
Total: 51 (1) games, 28 goals

2004/05
Newcastle United – 14th in Premiership
manager Bobby Robson, then Graeme Souness
League: 26 (2) games, 7 goals
FA Cup: 4 games, 1 goal
League Cup: 1 game, 0 goals
Europe: 9 games, 11 goals
Total: 40 (2) games, 19 goals

2005/06
Newcastle United
manager Graeme Souness, then Glenn Roeder
League: 31 (1) games, 10 goals
FA Cup: 3 games, 1 goal
League Cup: 2 games, 1 goal
Inter-Toto Cup : 4 games, 2 goals
Total: 40 (1) games, 15 goals

CLUB SUMMARY

SOUTHAMPTON
League: 105 (13) games, 23 goals
FA Cup: 11 (3) games, 4 goals
League Cup: 16 (2) games, 11 goals
Zenith Data Systems Cup: 8 games, 5 goals
Total: 140 (18) games, 43 goals

BLACKBURN ROVERS
League: 132 (6) games, 112 goals
FA Cup: 8 games, 2 goals
League Cup: 16 games, 14 goals
Europe: 8 games, 2 goals
Charity Shield: 1 game, 0 goals
Total: 165 (6) games, 130 goals

NEWCASTLE UNITED
League: 295 (8) games, 148 goals
FA Cup 36 games, 21 goals
League Cup: 15 (1) games, 7 goals
Europe: 45 games, 28 goals
Inter-Toto Cup: 4 games, 2 goals
Charity Shield: 1 game, 0 goals
Total: 396 (9) games, 206 goals

OVERALL CLUB RECORD
League: 532 (27) games, 283 goals
FA Cup: 55 (3) games, 27 goals
League Cup: 47 (3) games, 32 goals
Europe: 53 games, 30 goals
Inter-Toto Cup: 4 games, 2 goals
Charity Shield: 2 games, 0 goals
Zenith Data Systems Cup: 8 games, 5 goals
Total: 701 (33) games, 379 goals

SENIOR INTERNATIONAL CAREER

WCF = World Cup Finals,
WCQ = World Cup Qualifier,
ECF = European Championships Finals,
ECQ = European Championships Qualifier,
Fr = Friendly,
UI = Umbro International,
T = Tournoi.

63 ENGLAND CAPS, 30 GOALS

England 2 France 0 at Wembley (Fr), 19 February 2002, 1 goal
CIS 2 England 2 in Moscow (Fr), 29 April 1992
England 0 France 0 in Malmo (ECF), 14 June 1992
Spain 1 England 0 in Santander (Fr), 9 September 1992
England 1 Norway 1 at Wembley (WCQ), 14 October 1992
England 4 Turkey 0 at Wembley (WCQ), 18 November 1992, 1 goal
Holland 2 England 0 in Rotterdam (WCQ), 13 October 1993
England 1 Denmark 0 at Wembley (Fr), 9 March 1994
England 5 Greece 0 at Wembley (Fr), 17 May 1994, 1 goal
England 0 Norway 0 at Wembley (Fr), 22 May 1994
England 2 USA 0 at Wembley (Fr), 7 September 1994, 2 goals
England 1 Romania 1 at Wembley (Fr), 12 October 1994
England 1 Nigeria 0 at Wembley (Fr), 16 November 1994
Republic of Ireland 1 England 0 in Dublin (Fr, abandoned) 15 February 1995
England 2 Japan 1 at Wembley (UI), 3 June 1995
England 3 Sweden 3 at Elland Road (UI), 8 June 1995
England 1 Brazil 3 at Wembley (UI), 11 June 1995
England 0 Colombia 0 at Wembley (Fr), 6 September 1995
Norway 0 England 0 in Oslo (Fr), 11 October 1995
England 3 Switzerland 1 at Wembley (Fr), 15 November 1995
England 1 Portugal 1 at Wembley (Fr), 12 December 1995
England 3 Hungary 0 at Wembley (Fr), 18 May 1996
China 0 England 3 in Beijing (Fr), 23 May 1996
England 1 Switzerland 1 at Wembley (ECF), 8 June 1996, 1 goal
England 2 Scotland 0 at Wembley (ECF), 15 June 1996, 1 goal
England 4 Holland 1 at Wembley (ECF), 18 June 1996, 2 goals
England 0 Spain 0 at Wembley (ECF), 22 June 1996
England 1 Germany 1 at Wembley (ECF), 26 June 1996, 1 goal
Moldova 0 England 3 in Chisinau (WCQ), 1 September 1996, 1 goal
England 2 Poland 1 at Wembley (WCQ), 9 October 1996, 2 goals
England 0 Italy 1 at Wembley (WCQ), 12 February 1997
England 2 Georgia 0 at Wembley (WCQ), 30 April 1997, 1 goal
Poland 0 England 2 in Katowice (WCQ), 31 May 1997, 1 goal
France 0 England 1 in Montpellier (T), 7 June 1997, 1 goal
Brazil 1 England 0 in Paris (T), 10 June 1997
England 0 Chile 2 at Wembley (Fr), 11 February 1998
Switzerland 1 England 1 in Berne (Fr), 25 March 1998
England 3 Portugal 0 at Wembley (Fr), 22 April 1998, 2 goals
England 0 Saudi Arabia 0 at Wembley (Fr), 23 May 1998
England 2 Tunisia 0 in Marseille (WCF), 15 June 1998, 1 goal
England 1 Romania 2 in Toulouse (WCF), 22 June 1998
England 2 Colombia 0 in Lens (WCF), 26 June 1998
England 2 Argentina 0 in St Etienne (WCF), 30 June 1998, 1 goal
Sweden 2 England 1 in Stockholm (ECQ), 5 September 1998, 1 goal
England 0 Bulgaria 0 at Wembley (ECQ), 10 October 1998
Luxembourg 0 England 3 in Luxembourg (ECQ), 14 October 1998, 1 goal
England 0 France 2 at Wembley (Fr), 10 February 1999
England 3 Poland 1 at Wembley (ECQ), 27 March 1999

Hungary 1 England 1 in Budapest (Fr), 28 April 1999, 1 goal
England 0 Sweden 0 at Wembley (ECQ), 5 June 1999
Bulgaria 1 England 1 in Sofia (ECQ), 9 June 1999, 1 goal
England 6 Luxembourg 0 at Wembley (ECQ), 4 September 1999, 3 goals
Poland 0 England 0 in Warsaw (ECQ), 8 September 1999
England 2 Belgium 1 at Stadium of Light (Fr), 10 October 1999, 1 goal
Scotland 0 England 2 at Hampden Park (ECQ), 13 November 1999
England 0 Scotland 1 at Wembley (ECQ), 17 November 1999
England 0 Argentina 0 at Wembley (Fr), 23 February 2000
England 1 Brazil 1 at Wembley (Fr), 27 March 2000
England 2 Ukraine 0 at Wembley (Fr), 31 May 2000
Malta 1 England 2 in Valletta (Fr), 3 June 2000
England 2 Portugal 3 in Eindhoven (ECF), 12 June 2000
England 1 Germany 0 in Charleroi (ECF), 17 June 2000, 1 goal
England 2 Romania 3 in Charleroi (ECF), 20 June 2000, 1 goal

Alan Shearer also scored 11 goals in 13 appearances for England under-21s, and played once for England 'B'.

FOOTBALL HONOURS:
FWA Footballer of the Year 94;
PFA Footballer of the Year 95, 97;
Premiership title 94/5;
Premiership runner-up 93/4, 96/7;
FA Cup runner-up 98, 99;
Euro 96 Golden Boot;
Premiership Golden Boot 94/5, 95/6, 96/7;
Premiership Hall of Fame 94/5;
Premiership Player of Decade 99-02;

PERSONAL HONOURS:
OBE June 2001;
Freedom of City of Newcastle 2002.

TRANSFER FEES:
£3.6 million (Southampton to Blackburn Rovers in July 1992);
£15.6 million (Blackburn Rovers to Newcastle United in July 1996).

INDEX

ALAN SHEARER'S ACKNOWLEDGEMENTS

Thanks very much to all those who gave up their time so generously to get this book on the shelves. In particular, I would like to say how grateful I am to my 'Team of Life' at WMG Management – Helene Hollier in the office who has been like my right arm. Simon Bayliff whose friendship, support and help have been invaluable through the years (you played well to talk me into this!). Tony Stephens, of course, whose constant guidance and professional advice through the highs and lows of my career, has made many of these memories possible.

The only man for the job of ghost writing this book is my long-time trusted friend and 'journo hack' Dave Harrison, who knows me so well.

To Iain MacGregor for his help with logistics and producing the end result and to all at Cassell Illustrated for their professionalism and energy in making this right.

Finally, and most importantly, I would like to dearly thank my family for allowing me to dig out all of our old photos and memories for this book.

Photography supplied courtesy of Alan Shearer with the following exceptions:

Action Images 50 top left, 54 bottom left, 62 top, 68, 72-73, 85, 130 top, 139, 140; /Roy Beardsworth 50 bottom right; /Dan Chung/Reuters 98-99; /David Davies 194-195; /Film 53; /Stuart Franklin 98; /Nick Kidd/Sporting Images 75, 84; /Steve Morton 189; /Phil O'Connor/Sporting Pictures 52; /JM/HP/ Reuters 192 left; /KC/JES/Reuters 106 top; /KC/KM/ Reuters 100-101, 103; /Nigel Roddis/Reuters 222; /John Sibley 160 bottom right, 187 top, 224 bottom right, 235, 236; /John Sibley/Livepic 233; /Lee Smith endpapers, 130 bottom right; /Lee Smith/Livepic 134, 147 top, 147 bottom; /Jim Steele 74 bottom left; /Darren Walsh 62 centre, 142-143, 187 bottom. Colorsport 179; /Stuart MacFarlane 94. Southern Daily Echo 42-43, 83; /Southampton FC 138; /Southern Newspapers 34 top, 51. Empics 62 bottom, 172, 178, 197; /Matthew Ashton 118 bottom right, 154; /Adam Butler 86-87, 90, 104-105, 107; /Peter Byrne 238, 239; /Adam Davy 126; /Mike Egerton 95 bottom, 122 right, 129 right, 146-147, 153 top right; /John Giles 70-71, 119, 123, 144, 173, 176, 193 right, 219 bottom; /Laurence Griffiths 74 top, 89, 175; /David Hewitson 161, 168-169, 174; /Owen Humphreys 2 centre, 111, 130 bottom left, 153 top left, 180-181, 183, 202-203, 204, 230-231, 247; /Ross Kinnaird 54 top, 54 bottom right, 64-65, 67, 70 top left, 155; /Tony Marshall 2 top left, 95 top, 177, 185 top; /Rebecca Naden 2 centre left, 108 right; /Phil Noble 127, 128; /Nick Potts 116 right; /Brian Rasmussen/Scanpix 118 bottom left; /Peter Robinson 74 bottom right, 92-93, 156; /S&G/Alpha 14 bottom right, 30, 31; /Neal Simpson 50 top right, 108 left, 122 left; /Michael Steele 125, 180; /Michael Stephens 224 top, 241; /John Stillwell 210-211; /Darren Walsh/Chelsea FC 124 left; /John Walton 129 left. Getty Images/Allsport 191; /Odd Andersen/AFP 118 top; /Bongarts 88, 153 bottom right; /Justin Bond/AFP 182; /Shaun Botterill 2 bottom left, 112; /Shaun Botterill/Allsport 91 left, 91 right, 186; /Marcus Brandt/Bongarts 11; /Clive Brunskill/Allsport 70 centre left, 131, 150-151, 160 bottom left, 185 bottom; /David Cannon/Allsport 157, 158; /Paul Ellis/AFP 136-137, 148-149, 219 top; /Stu Forster 148; /Stu Forster/Allsport 188, 194; /Laurence Griffiths 205, 208-209, 214 right, 215; /Laurence Griffiths/Allsport 109 top; /Boris Horavt 102; /Ian Horrocks/Newcastle United 160 top, 214 left, 216, 217, 220-221, 223, 229; /Ross Kinnaird/Allsport 2 top left, 2 bottom centre, 106 centre, 106 bottom, 116 left, 117; /Matthew Lewis 218; /Alex Livesey 2 centre right; /Clive First Mason/Allsport 192 right, 193 left; /Steve Powell/Allsport 159; /Gary M. Prior 232; /Gary M. Prior/Allsport 109 bottom, 141, 198-199, 200-201; /Ben Radford 2 top centre, 145; /David Rogers 7; /Carl De Souza/AFP 153 bottom left; /Serena Taylor/Newcastle United 13, 227, 234, 236-237; /Mark Thompson 124 right. News International Syndication/The Sun 34 bottom right, 49, 55, 61, 63, 69; /The Times 110. Popperfoto 97. Rex Features 170-171. TopFoto/Topham/Pro Sport 114.

Published in Great Britain in 2007 by Cassell Illustrated, a division of Octopus Publishing Group Limited, 2-4 Heron Quays, London E14 4JP

Text copyright © 2007 Alan Shearer
Design and layout © Octopus Publishing Group

A CIP catalogue record for this book is available from the British Library.

ISBN-13: 1-84403-586-7

10 9 8 7 6 5 4 3 2 1

Printed in England by Butler and Tanner, Frome

Text: Alan Shearer with Dave Harrison
Publisher: Iain MacGregor
Editor: Jo Wilson
Design: ASH
Picture research: Jennifer Veall